THE
RE...
ROUTE GUIDE

EXCELLENT BOOKS

EXCELLENT BOOKS
94 BRADFORD ROAD
WAKEFIELD
WEST YORKSHIRE WF1 2AE
TEL / FAX: (01924) 315147

First Published 1999

ISBN 1-901464-05-9
Whilst the author has cycled and researched the route for the purposes of this guide, no responsibility can be accepted for any unforeseen circumstances encountered whilst following it. The publisher would, however, welcome information regarding any material changes and problems encountered.

Front cover photo: Kielder Forest
Rear cover photo: Kielder Forest
Frontispiece: Looking towards Whitley Bay

Printed in Great Britain by:
FM Repro Ltd.
Repro House, 69 Lumb Lane
Roberttown
Liversedge
West Yorkshire WF15 7NB

CONTENTS

Bridge on the cycle path heading towards Wide Open (section 1)

INTRODUCTION

WHAT IS THE REIVERS?

The Reivers Cycle Route encompasses almost 190 miles of cycle paths, tracks and minor roads from Newcastle, across Northumberland to Kielder, then through historic Carlisle to Whitehaven on the west coast. It was generated in part by the immense success of the C2C cycle route, the brainchild of the cycling and path-building charity Sustrans; the thousands of cyclists who completed this route every year generated a demand for a return route, so they could travel back to their start point via new scenery and take on a fresh challenge! It is also, of course, a route in its own right.

The route's title is borrowed from the lawless border families of the 16th century; to reive is to pillage and reiving was especially associated with the raiding of cattle. Such raids were largely organised by extended border families and it was usually other border families who were the victims. Much of the landscape must have changed little since these unforgiving times and it is easy to see how it was so difficult for any central authority to exert control over quick-moving horse mounted raiders in this vast landscape.

Add to this rich pattern of history the fact that you pass through the Northumberland and Lake District National Parks as well as the Border Forest Park and you have an unbeatable combination!

WHAT TO EXPECT

This is undoubtedly a challenging route; it is some 50 miles longer than the C2C and although it doesn't get above 400 metres (the C2C climbs to over 500m) it involves some similarly stiff climbs, most notably between Kielder and Newcastleton and crossing the Caldbeck Fells. The real answer is not to try hard to maintain your speed on these climbs but to take them at your own pace and allow extra time to take in the stunning scenery. Route profiles at the start of each chapter should be studied carefully to give you a specific idea of what to expect.

If completing the route from east to west (the intended direction as a return C2C route) be aware that you will be cycling into the prevailing winds; this means The Reivers is very much a summer route (or an out of seaon one also if you can be ready at short notice to head off on windless days).

Although physically challenging, the route has been designed to be safe and easy to follow, although you should plan well and take plenty of food and appropriate clothing when crossing the exposed middle sections. The following features make it especially suitable for leisure riders and some sections are also ideal for mountain bikers.

• **Off-road sections.** A significant proportion of the route uses either dedicated off-road cycle tracks or bridleway. This is especially so at either end of the route and around Kielder (the best area for 'pure' mountain biking).

• **Waymarking**. The route is well signed - see the sign on the front of this book for the main route sign. In addition, most off-road options have their own route sign as shown overleaf. Occasionally a white painted stencil is also used on the ground. The directions given on the maps should confirm route signs and will help if they are missing or vandalised.

• **Avoids traffic**. When not off-road the route uses quiet country lanes where possible. The guide alerts you to any small sections of busy or major road and gives suitable advice on minimising risk (this only happens very occasionally).

MAIN BIKE TRAILS USED BY THE REIVERS

North Shields - Backworth Waggonway Once a rail line taking coal to the coast, this now takes you away from the heart of the urban area to former mining communities on its edge.

Kielder Water Cycle Circuit Should you choose the off-road option along the northern shore of the reservoir you will be following signs for Kielder cycle route number 6, one of a great number of signed cycle routes around the forest. There is also the chance to use parts of the differently lettered options of route 5 to get to Akenshaw.

Workington to Camerton Path

5km of easy cycle path. It is also part of the West Cumbria Cycle Network and Sustrans National Route 7.

Combined C2C National Route 7 and Reivers route sign near Carlisle

Reivers off-road option sign which also follows Kielder cycle route 5a.

SUSTRANS - THE CYCLE PATH CHARITY

Sustrans is short for sustainable transport and it is through the construction of an 8,000 mile National Cycle Network that this organisation hopes to promote this aim. Since its founding in 1980 Sustrans has seen a spectacular growth in popularity. Over £40 million of Millennium funds have been earmarked to help in the construction of this cycle network. Sustrans aims to promote local journeys by bike and 'green tourism'. Sustrans also relies on income from members. For further details of Sustrans services contact:

SUSTRANS HEAD OFFICE
35 King Street, Bristol BS1 4DZ
(0117) 929 0888

ROUTE GEOGRAPHY AND HISTORY - AN OVERVIEW

THE INFLUENCE OF BORDERS HISTORY

Both Northumbria and northern Cumbria have been greatly affected by a turbulent history of border unrest. The area already had a long tradition of warfare when the Normans arrived here in the 11th century, and proceeded to build castle strongholds such as that at Carlisle. The initial Norman truce with Scotland was only temporary and intermittent warfare continued for the next 630 years or so. Edward I, William Wallace, Robert the Bruce, Flodden Edge, Mary Stuart, the Old Pretender and the Young Pretender are simply some of the more famous names that epitomise hostility between England and Scotland over the centuries. Quite often in the game of European politics Scotland found itself lining up with France against England.

The reiving families from either side of the border most probably viewed national and international politics as potentially obstructive to their preferred activities of cattle rustling and exacting material advantage from other families by whatever method they could. After James V of Scotland and several English Wardens of the Marches, appointed by the king to keep peace in the area, failed to subdue the reivers their downfall came with the Union of the Crowns under James I in 1603. He pursued them mercilessly, hanging many of them and disarming the border area.

This past lawlessness has left its mark on many of the fortified buildings you pass on the route; good examples are the Vicar's Pele tower at Ponteland, Askerton Castle (a fortified residence on section 5), Carlisle Castle and the fortified church tower in Burgh by Sands but these are just a few of the many scores you pass near along the way.

FROM THE COAST TO BELLINGHAM

The long sandy beaches stretching from Tynemouth up to Whitley Bay could not present more of a contrast to the post- industrial hinterland you pass through between North Shields and Wide Open. Many traces of Tyneside's proud traditions of shipbuilding and coal mining remain. There are great views over the Tyne at the very start of the route, and many great ships once sailed out to sea from here after being constructed on the river banks. Former mining settlements are then very much in evidence; you pass old slag heaps near Backworth and Burradon that are only now beginning to take on a grassy cover.

NORTHUMBERLAND NATIONAL PARK AND THE WESTERN BORDERS

Rolling upland scenery dominates the route from around Stamfordham and into the Northumberland National Park at Bellingham. Villages are few, perhaps a legacy of the area's violent and unsettled past, and wide horizons dominate. Upland streams or burns feed the broad and serene River North Tyne, whose banks you run alongside for several kilometres below Falstone.

After the dense blanket of Forestry Commission trees around Kielder, the Border region south of Newcastleton and down to Bewcastle has some of the wildest, loneliest landscapes in the whole of our islands. The vast swathes of Kielder conifers have disappeared and the exposed moorland hereabouts is characterised by high rainfall and poor drainage, giving rise to some boggy pasture, dissected by a number of unpolluted streams and rivers. The disappearance of much of the traditional cover of birch and alder has only served to emphasise the area's beautiful desolation.

Gourmets wanting Northumbrian food may want to sample a stotty sandwich, a round flat loaf that can be filled with local cheese such as Redesdale or Cotherstone. Local breweries include Longstone, Butterknowle and Big Lamp.

THE RIVER EDEN AND NORTHERN LAKE DISTRICT

Where the Eden touches the Reivers at Rockliffe and Carlisle it is still a broad river; to the west of Carlisle it has spilled out into the muddy flats of the Solway Firth, an area rich in birdlife. Miles of plain, dotted with quiet villages, give good views over the firth to the Southern Uplands of Scotland.

Heading south the broken mass of the northern tip of the Lake District looms up. Away from the tourist 'honeypots' of the central Lakes the quiet expanses of the Caldbeck and Uldale Fells are backed by yet higher peaks such as the imposing Skiddaw, one of Lakeland's highest peaks at over 3,000 feet. Streams tumble over rocky descents, such as Dash Beck a few kilometres before Bassenthwaite village on the off-road option.

THE WEST COAST

Although the West Cumbrian coast admittedly lacks the sandy beauty of the east coast, the working town of Workington and the industrial remains on a spectacular coastal path approaching Whitehaven give it a different but equally appealing feel. Whitehaven's well-preserved Georgian architecture is a unique end point to the route.

GETTING THERE AND AWAY

Arrive by train! This is the message Sustrans are trying to get across and rightly so. There are potential problems in taking bikes on trains (space is often limited on main lines where bikes are put in separate coaches and on branch lines usually you must simply wait and see if there is space in one of the normal carriages), but with a little planning you shouldn't have any trouble. Privatisation has also lead to divergence in rules about carrying bikes on trains; some carriers may make a great effort to accommodate you whilst others might have unhelpful restrictions. The best rules are to **book ahead as early as possible** on main line journeys and on branch lines get to the guard as quickly as possible! In practice problems are likely to arise either in the morning or evening 'rush hour' when little space is available, and even here the density of passengers varies dramatically depending on the particular journey. A summary of the present situation follows but you always check up-to-date arrangements.

• On Inter-City journeys from the rest of the UK to Newcastle bike reservations are necessary and generally cost £3. Again check details of your particular journey.
• For a summary of stations around the route see the map overleaf. Bike policies of the train companies operating in the area of The Reivers are as follows:

Northern Spirit (Newcastle to Carlisle) Up to 2 bikes per train, generally non-reservable. There are a few services that are reservable; phone for details. Enquiries (0870) 6023322
North West Trains (Whitehaven and Workington to Carlisle) 2 spaces available, non-reservable, on a 'first come first served'basis. Enquiries (0870) 6066007

NOTE The link shown on the map to Tynemouth and Whitley Bay is part of the 'metro' system and at the time of writing bikes were not allowed on it. (NEXUS Travel Line (0191) 2325325). If you arrive in Newcastle by train you can cycle along the last part of the C2C to Tynemouth.

0345 484950 - RAIL ENQUIRIES

The above number is excellent for getting straightforward fare and timetable information. However, beware when asking for particular information on taking bikes on trains. Very general advice is often given and is not necessarily accurate! They may simply give you the number for the operating company concerned; in any case this is the best advice; you are better getting particular details from the operators, who will be more precise.

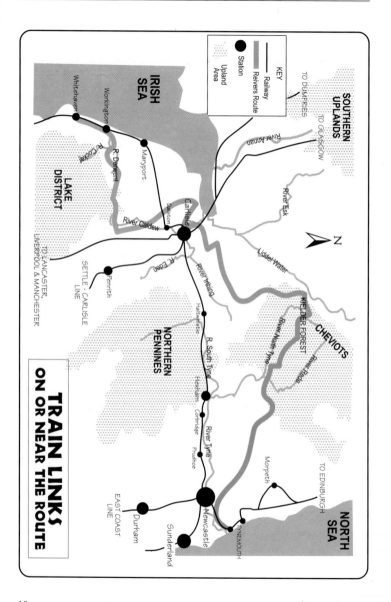

TRAIN LINKS
ON OR NEAR THE ROUTE

10

PREPARATION

The Reivers is probably of about the same level of difficulty as the Sustrans C2C, which has an official rating of 'challenging' (the most difficult rating is 'very challenging' and this is applied to the Welsh National Route). Although it doesn't climb to quite the same heights as the C2C it is some 50 miles longer and there is the chance that you'll be cycling into the prevailing winds (see page 4 for more information on this).

Despite the challenging and remote nature of some of the upland terrain, like the C2C, it is a leisure route completed by a wide range of people of varying ages. Being a Sustrans Regional Route means that whilst it is not directly managed and officially mapped by Sustrans it is run by local authorities or similar organisations on the ground who are responsible for maintenance and signposting. There is a route map, available through Sustrans, and this is an invaluable addition to this guide.

The guide splits the route into 7 'day sections' ranging from 20 miles (section 3) to 36.5 miles (section 7), but the latter is easily spilt into two shorter day rides by stopping in Cockermouth. Sections 4 and 6 are undoubtedly the toughest. Allowing for travelling time and a couple of rest days the whole route makes a stunning 10 day holiday. Some keen cyclists, especially those with previous experience of the route, can complete it much more quickly. Of course, it can also be cycled on a section by section basis using free weekends.

Section start and finish points are as near as possible to centres of population where accommodation is plentiful, but this is not always possible when trying to keep section distances reasonably even. It is still advisable to book accommodation as far in advance as practicable; this is especially the case if you are completing the route in summer or you are planning to stay in smaller settlements with only limited accommodation. This is particularly important on the sparsely populated sections 3,4 and 5. Those wanting to camp along the way should certainly have some previous cycling experience and allow extra time as the extra equipment weight slows down even the fittest cyclist quite noticeably.

One of the most important factors in preparation is to have a realistic idea of what daily mileage you are comfortable in achieving; a number of shorter 'dry-runs' nearer to home, over varying terrain and in varying weather conditions, will help immensely in giving you an accurate idea of your capabilities.

11

CHECKLIST   Basic essentials - there is a huge range of specialist cycling gear available. The list assumes you are staying B&B (i.e. not camping).

Clothing (winter / summer options included)
Helmet
High wicking inner layer (doesn't soak up sweat)
Cycle shirt and / or fleece top
Waterproof outer (preferably breathable-
well known makes are Goretex and Ceplex)
Gloves
Padded shorts
Thermal leggings
Tracksuit bottoms
Waterproof trousers
Boots / trainers / cycling shoes
At the least one change of clothing based
on the above
Sun hat / glasses / block

**Tool Kit ('Multi-tools' may
include several of these)**
Small screwdriver
Small adjustable spanner
Allen keys (4,5,6 mm at least)
Pump
Spare brake blocks
Strong tape for quick repair
Small container of chain and gear lubricant
Chain link extractor
Puncture kit & new inner tubes

Other Essentials
Guide and maps (see section on map use)
Water bottle
Telephone contact of friends/family for emergency
Toilet paper
Survival bag (used to keep warm if stuck in foul weather conditions)

Bike lights
Money
Washing kit
Towel
Small first aid kit
Prescribed medication

BACKUP SERVICES - SEE PAGE 81
Useful services include resue call-out, cycle lock-ups and luggage transfer.

MAINTENANCE

If you set off with a well-maintained bike the chances are that you won't need any of the tools or spares you take. A bike in good condition is especially important for such a long distance route. The most basic check should include the following list and if in any doubt about the state of your bike get it checked over properly at a good bike shop.

Important safety checks - do not neglect them!

Brake check - you should only be able to squeeze in front and rear brake levers a centimetre or two and braking response should be nice and sharp. Check brake blocks aren't rubbing on wheel rims, or even worse, tyres.

Brake cables - check that front and rear brake cables are not fraying. If they are replace them immediately.

Brake blocks - check that when you brake the blocks hit only the wheel rim, not the tyre and that there is plenty of wear left in the block.

Tyres - should be inflated to manufacturer's recommended pressure (as a rough guide you should just be able to depress the tyre when squeezing it). Check there is adequate tread.

Make sure the following are **lubricated**: front and rear brake pivots, moving parts of front and rear gear mechanisms, chain, brake lever pivots, entry and exit points of all cables. Keep these points well-lubricated during the ride.

Appropriate **screws and bolts** should be tight and you should check all gears are shifting properly.

For a full guide to buying and maintaining a bike see Haynes 'The Bike Book'.

CARRYING LOADS

Panniers are the ideal way to carry your extra gear. Small amounts of gear can be put in bum bags and the smaller seat and frame bags that fit around the bike or in handlebar bags or even a very small backpack. However, unless travelling very light in summer, you will probably need panniers. Start off with rear panniers which sit on a frame over the rear wheel. Large amounts of extra gear will go in 'low rider' front panniers either side of the front forks. At all costs don't overload handlebar bags or a backpack - this will dangerously affect handling and balance.

Sheepmount Bridge, heading out of Carlisle (section 6)

SIGNING & STAMPING

Waymarking as shown on the front cover is apparent at most junctions of the main route, with a special off-road sign being used on many of the off-road options (see pages 5 and 6 for photos). Directions given on the maps in this book are especially useful to confirm your direction in case of confusion; sometimes the exact direction of a route sign may be unclear or it may have been twisted around, stolen or vandalised!

A stamping card comes with the route map available from Sustrans and when completed provides documentary proof of your journey! There are 4 stamping points detailed on the card, at Tynemouth, Kielder Water (Leaplish), Carlisle and Whitehaven.

USING THIS GUIDE AND OTHER MAPS

Although you should be able to complete The Reivers with an up-to-date edition of this book you are strongly advised to take other maps. You should, at least, take the Reivers route map. A further but bulky and expensive addition would be the 8 OS Landranger maps (1:50,000 scale) listed below. These contain more detail over a wider area and are the best maps if you want to go exploring off the main route.

No. 88 - Newcastle upon Tyne
No. 87 - Hexham & Haltwhistle
No. 80 - Cheviot Hills and Kielder Forest
No. 79 - Hawick and Eskdale
No. 86 - Haltwhistle & Brampton
No. 85 - Carlisle & Solway Firth
No. 90 - Pentith & Keswick
No. 89 - West Cumbria

MAP KEY

Reivers Bike Route - Main route/ off-road option	River / canal
Motorway / trunk road	Railway
A-road / B-road / minor road	
Settlement	Track / off-road

B&B / CAMPSITE KEY

Information is based on individual questionnaires from owners; please confirm the information before booking. Other accommodation providers are listed with briefer details where they have not returned questionnaires. Brief details are also given of camping sites indicated by a △ sign in the text.

B&B Abbreviations - prices are per person per night based on a double room.

£ = Under £10   ££ = Under £15   £££ = Under £20   ££££ = Under £25
£££££ = Over £25   PL = Packed Lunches (other meals also detailed) DR = Drying Facilities LAU = Laundry Facilities SEC = Secure Bike Place WKSH = Workshop Facilities.

Bikers at Dalston (section 6)

1 TYNEMOUTH - STAMFORDHAM

Section Distance 25.5 miles / 41km   **Off-road** 13.5 miles / 22km

The Route After a spectacular start along the Tyne estuary you turn inland through housing estates to join an old waggonway track, once used for transporting coal. This industry has now left, and the more usual modern industries based on trading estates have come to replace it. There are some reminders in the form of disused collieries and old spoil heaps. Although the Whitley Bay alternative route is more picturesque, giving you the chance to see some lovely beaches and to visit Whitley Bay itself, it was not signed at the time of writing and the initial section uses some busy roads. The gradients on both options are very even.

ALTERNATIVE START THROUGH WHITLEY BAY

• **Whitley Bay** is one of Tyneside's favourite seaside resorts, blessed with a large sandy beach and the traditional guest houses and amusement arcades (Spanish City amusement park, with its White Moorish Dome, is a listed building). Low tide gives the opportunity to walk out to **St Mary's Island** at the north end of the sands, with a pretty group of houses and a lighthouse that houses a museum and spectacular viewpoint. Opening hours depend on the tide! Admission charge. (0191) 2008650. Barclays and Natwest banks with cashpoints on different branches of Park View. **Tourist Information**, Park Road (0191) 2008535.
• **Cullercoats** was once a fishing village but is now absorbed by Whitley Bay. Its little harbour and sandy bay remain. ACCOMMODATION NOTE There is so much accommodation in Whitley Bay no attempt has been made to cover it. Outside of very peak season there should be no availability problems.

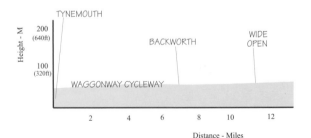

TYNEMOUTH TO STAMFORDHAM

• **Tynemouth Priory and Castle**, surrounded by curiously eroded gravestones, overlooks your starting point by the pier. Originally an 11th century Norman church and developed within a castle enclosure. Percy Chantry is the only complete part left (heavily restored). English Heritage site. April-Oct open daily. Nov-March Weds to Sun. Coastguard's regional H.Q. lies alongside. The **Volunteer Life Brigade Museum** is just above the start point and recounts daring tales of rescue. Closed Mon and Sunday afternoons. (0191) 2572059. The **Sea Life Centre** on Grand Parade has real life sharks and rays. Open daily. Admission charge. (0191) 2581031.**Childhood Memories Toy Museum** is at Palace Buildings (0191) 2590905. There is a branch of Barclays on Front St. with cashpoint.

• **Collingwood Monument** This native of Newcastle took command of the fleet at Trafalgar and continues to look over the mouth of the Tyne today.

• **Black Middens** Once notorious rocks near the Tyne entrance. Claimed 5 ships in 3 days in November 1864.

• **Clifford's Fort** near the Fish Quay is the remains of a seventeenth century armed fort named after Lord Clifford of Cabal. Passing through the quayside area of **North Shields** two white towers above and on the quay are navigational aids that ships could use to aid a safe passage up the Tyne (done by aligning them). There are far fewer trawlers use the fish quay now than a century ago when North Shields saw its heyday but there are, nonetheless, many fish & chip shops!

• **Royal Quays** An enormous shopping and housing redevelopment area. Look out for the viewpoint in Redburn Dene park. **Wet n' Wild** is a tropical indoor water park en route. (0191) 2961333. **Tourist Information** is opposite the Reivers at Coble Dene, Royal Quays. (0191) 2005895.

• A waggonway cycleway takes you away from the Tyne passing the **Stephenson Railway Museum** which exhibits pioneer steam locomotives. The Stephensons came from nearby Killingworth and figure largely here. Trips on steam railway that runs alongside the Reivers waggonway track. (0191) 2007145.

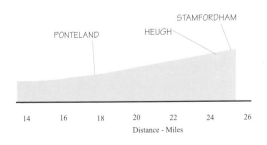

• The **Bay Horse** at Dinnington serves bar meals all day and is open from 11.20 on weekdays and 12.00 on Sundays.

• The countryside gradually takes over from the urban development of North Tyneside before you enter **Ponteland**. Once an old village, a new housing estate aimed to make this an upmarket dormitory settlement for Newcastle workers has been added. The **Blackbird Inn** is a restored 17th century manor house, itself built onto a 14th century pele tower. Drinks served in the 600 year old basement plus all day food. The Diamond Inn also serves food. Lloyds, Midlands, Barclays, Natwest and Link cashpoints along the main street.

• **Stamfordham** is a beautiful example of a planned eighteenth century estate village, centred around a green, village cross, pond and lock-up (once used if visiting drovers became too rowdy!). Once part owned by local nobility and Balliol College, Oxford. Pretty path across River Pont to hamlet of Hawkwell. **Stamfordham Gallery**, Old Barclays Bank. Temporary exhibitions and permanent collection. **Bay Horse** and **Swinburne Arms** pubs. Latter does meals 12-3 and 7-10.30 and has real ales.

TYNEMOUTH TO STAMFORDHAM - ACCOMMODATION

Northumberland Bothy, Tynemouth Station (01830) 540342 and (0191) 2583167. £(£) PL-DR-LAU-SEC. Bunk beds, showers, toilets and bike store. Bedding available. Stamping point. Open April-Nov. Coffee shop opposite.
The 61, 61 Front St. Tynemouth (0191) 2573687
Hope House, 47 Percy Gardens, Tynemouth (0191) 2571989
Grand Hotel, Grand Parade, Tynemouth (0191) 2936666
Park Hotel, Grand Parade, Tynemouth (0191) 2571406
The Swallow Gosforth Park Hotel, Wide Open (0191) 2364111
7 Collingwood Cottages, Limestone Lane, Ponteland (01661) 825967. £££-PL-DR-LAU-SC-WKSH.
East Farm, Prestwick nr Ponteland)1661) 872480
The Diamond Inn, Ponteland (01661) 872898
Horton Grange Hotel, Berwick Hill, Ponteland (01661) 860686
Church House, South Side, Stamfordham (01661) 886736
The Bay Horse, Stamfordham, South Side (01661) 886244
⚠ **Whitley Bay Holiday Park**, The Links, Whitley Bay (0191) 2531216

Bridleway track approaching Backworth (section 1)

Path by the Tyne Estuary (section 1)

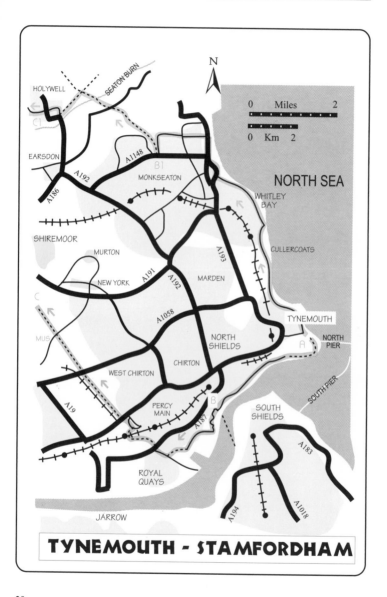

TYNEMOUTH - STAMFORDHAM

DIRECTION TIPS - MAIN ROUTE ALONG THE TYNE AND TO BACKWORTH

A - B Start in the car park by Tynemouth harbour. Go along the concrete path underneath the Collingwood Monument. After passing along the spectacular north bank of the Tyne go through the car park and bear R into the fish trading area and past the New Dolphin pub. Stay on this road alongside the Tyne as Union Road becomes Union Quay and New Quay. Pass the pedestrian ferry to South Shields then just past the Chain Locker pub go R up a ramp. After a small carry up steps bear L into housing estate (Tennyson Terrace). Head L down the next alley and L onto Addison St.

B - C Go over the crossroads and onto Lawson St. L at the end of Lawson St. and R at the next T-junction, to head towards the water chutes of Wet n' Wild on Robert Westall Way. Carry on at the end of the street onto the main cycle track through Red Dene Park. Meet the dual carriageway at Royal Quays shopping centre and turn R onto the cycle path, keeping the road on your L. Under a large road bridge the path splits. Go L to pass flats named after famous cricketers. After the flats go second R onto a tarmac path and follow under Metro line to emerge by the Percy Arms. Immediate R then L onto the road in front of Percy Main Community Centre. In about 30m head L and under the A193 onto the long, straight waggonway track next to the railtrack. Simply stay on this track, crossing over the first road you come to by the Stephenson Rail Museum, to continue on the waggonway.

DIRECTION TIPS - ALTERNATIVE ROUTE TO BACKWORTH VIA WHITLEY BAY
NOTE THAT AT THE TIME OF WRITING THIS ALTERNATIVE OPTION WAS UNSIGNED

A - B1 Follow the coast road north for about 5km then turn L onto Western Way. Cross over Claremont Rd onto Woodburn Drive. Pass the school on your R and go 90 degrees L and down Cragside to a junction with main road. Go R and in about 50m go R onto a bridleway track.

B1 - C1 Carry on, on this track on, under a small stone bridge. Cross over the small wooded valley of Seaton Burn and immediately under another small stone bridge go L onto a track. This turns into a road with houses. Turn R down the alley by the side of the Milbourne Arms and bear L Wylam Avenue, continuing to a T-junction with the main road. R onto the main road and first L down Tillmouth Av. Take the third L down Denham Drive and 10-15m post Stamford Av go L onto a footpath and bear R to exit the housing estate, crossing over a tarmac path and onto a wide earth track (CAN BE MUDDY!).

DIRECTION TIPS - MAIN ROUTE TO BACKWORTH

C - D Follow the waggonway track past an electricity substation and over two main roads at Shiremoor. Coming alongside a railway line on the L the track almost peters out. Bear R to a track T-junction and L. This turns into tarmac and at the next T-junction go L to enter Backworth over a level crossing. * At the next T-junction go R onto the B1322 and leave Backworth on this road.

D - E Follow this road until about 40m after passing the turning for the A1056 you head L onto a cinder track and under the A19. At the first crossroads carry straight on to join a new section of cyclepath and ascend to a good viewpoint. Descend, swinging to the L side of the pond and through an alley into houses. Head in a straight line through two cul-de-sacs to meet the B5015 by the Grey Horse Inn. Head straight over the road and follow the cinder track over a railway line and under a main raod to meet the B1319.Go R here and next L onto the bridleway signed for Wide Open.

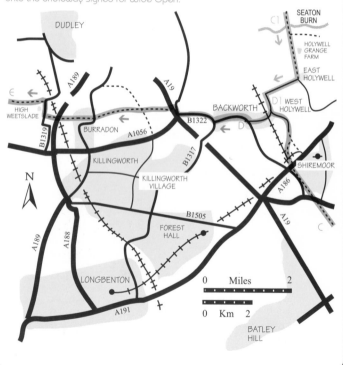

DIRECTION TIPS - ALTERNATIVE ROUTE VIA WHITLEY BAY

C1 - D1 On the track out of Holywell take the L-hand option and on meeting a better quality vehicle track go R. Shortly pass Holywell Grange Farm on the L and emerge at a road T-junction by a disused colliery. Go R and follow the road as it bends into Backworth, entering over the level-crossing. You are now back on the main route. Pick up directions at the point marked * on the facing page.

Looking back towards Whitley Bay from Burradon (section 1)

DIRECTION TIPS

E - F Pass through a field and onto a wide track by a large spoil heap on
your R (can be muddy). After passing over a small bridge go R at the next
split in the track and follow the track along the back of Wide Open until you
meet the road. Cross at the green cycle crossing and L onto the pavement cycle
lane. Just over a stream go R onto a tarmac track and in about 130m go R
over the main stream to come alongside a small stream. The track then bends
L to become tarmac again and crosses over the A1. Follow the road to its end
at North East Mason Farm and head straight on, onto a cinder track. Follow the
track to meet the road in Dinnington. Bear R past the estate roads of East and
West Acres to a T-junction with a main road and R (careful - fast traffic). Go
first L and onto a quiet minor road . Pass Carr Grange Farm and go R at the
first junction onto a long, straight but bumpy road.

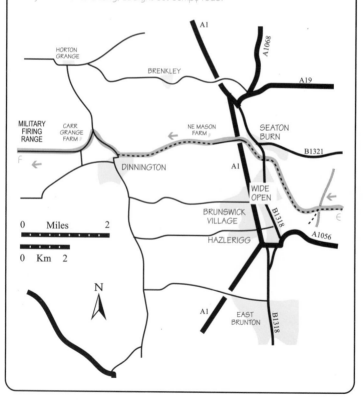

DIRECTION TIPS

F - G At the crossroads by Mayfair House go straight across. When the road finally ends keep on in a straight line onto the cinder track to come alongside a golf course. At the next track T-junction go L and bend through the pretty hamlet of Elland Hall. The track turns to tarmac and you enter Ponteland alongside the River Pont. At the crossroads with traffic lights head straight across onto the B6323. (Town centre to the R).

G - H In about 150m turn R onto the track signed for West Road. In 30-40m take two lefts in quick succession and onto a wider track through Darras Hall residential area. Straight over the first road and then follow through a small development of bungalows to another road. Jink L and R between a petrol station and a small row of shops to pick up the track again behind the latter. At the next road junction go R and in about 35m L onto The Crescent. In another 60-70m fork R onto a track. Follow this to a T-junction with a road and L. R at the next T-junction and pass Red House Farm on the R.

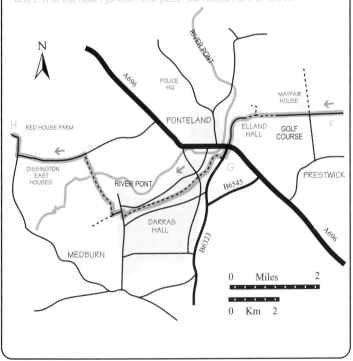

DIRECTION TIPS

H - I After passing Red House Farm take the next L, signed for Heugh and Stamfordham. Follow this road for about 2.5km to a T-junction with the B6309 and L. On entering Stamfordham take the first R, onto the village green area.

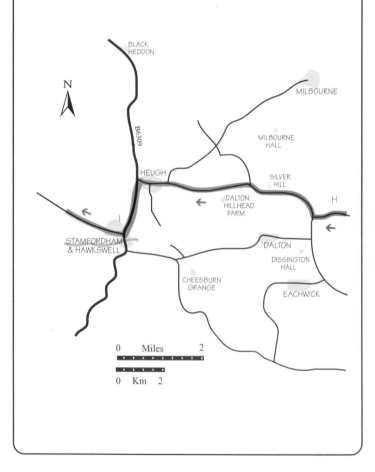

Cycle track near Burradon

2 STAMFORDHAM - BELLINGHAM

Section Distance 24.5 miles / 39km   **Off-road** 10 miles / 16km using
all possible off-road options

The Route The orderliness of beautiful estate villages such as Stamfordham and Matfen gives way to lonely, rolling moorland and hills become accordingly steeper before you drop down by the impressive River North Tyne just before Bellingham. It is possible to do the whole section on minor roads (some very minor and isolated indeed). Note there is no pub or cafe on the route between Matfen and Birtley, where there is a pub only, a distance of some 15 miles, so be well prepared. The detour to Wark is shown on the map as this provides handy shops, pubs and accommodation in a sparsely populated area.

STAMFORDHAM TO BELLINGHAM

• **Matfen** Immediately recognisable from the tall thin spire of Holy Trinity Church soaring through the trees. 19th century estate village of the Blackett family, set in scenic parkland. The large Matfen Hall is now a Chesire Home. The village is laid out harmoniously around a large green and gently flowing stream. **Black Bull Inn** serves food.
• **Throckrington** An isolated hamlet which you miss if you choose the off-road option in this area. Standing proud above the moorland, older remains around the centre were supposedly once deserted because of typhoid. Today it is reduced to a church and a group of farm buildings.

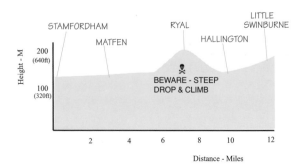

• **Wark**, a sizeable village for this remote area of Northumberland, is found several kilometres off the main route, on the link route to Haltwhistle, by the River North Tyne. Entry is over an impressive bridge. It was a frontier town in the Norman period but only the steep bank of its castle remains. A 16th century farmhouse can be found next to the main green. Also boasts an attractive mechanics' institute. The grand Chipchase Castle can be seen from the road here. Selection of pubs and hotels for food and drink.

• **Bellingham** Gateway to the relatively new landscape of reservoir and evergreen forest of Kielder country and pronounced 'Belling-jum'. The small market town is based around a wide main street with many attractive 19th century buildings. Barclays / Lloyds Banks on the main street, with cashpoints.

• The **Town Hall** boasts a Chinese musket from the Boxer Rebellion and a Boer War monument is next to it in the market place. Once a centre of coal and ironwork (some of the latter is said to grace the Tyne Bridge in Newcastle). Accommodation may be a problem in season as it is a well-established stop on the Pennine Way.

• **St Cuthbert's Church** has an unusual stone roof which was a defence against Scots raiders' attempts at arson. The 'long pack' grave here is associated with local legend. A path from the churchyard leads to Cuddy's Well. Beautiful walk up Hareshaw Burn to Hareshaw Linn waterfall.

• **The Heritage Centre** shows the history of the Border Counties Railway plus other aspects of local history. Seasonal opening. (01434) 220050.

• There is a **tourist information office** on Main Street (01434) 220616.

• The last part of this section and the first part of the next runs roughly parallel to the disused **Border Counties Line** and its overgrown bankings, bridges, cattle arches, sheep creeps and culverts are evident in many places. It began life in 1856, linking Hexham with an upland colliery, and was later extended to join the Scottish network at Riccarton. It proved economically viable for only a century.

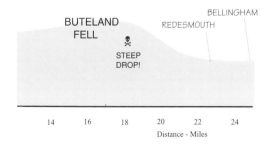

BUTELAND FELL

☠
STEEP DROP!

REDESMOUTH

BELLINGHAM

14   16   18   20   22   24

Distance - Miles

STAMFORDHAM TO BELLINGHAM - ACCOMMODATION

The Black Bull, Matfen (01661) 886330
The Tone Inn (01434) 270417. 0.5 miles north of the route on the A68.
Colt Crag Farm nr Birtley, Wark on Tyne (01434) 681419. £££-PL-DR-LAU-SEC. Dinner also available. Located as above, on the A68, but about 0.5 miles south of the route crossing of this main road.
The Black Bull, Wark (01434) 230239. £££££-PL-DR-LAU-SEC-some tools. Being refurbished at time of writing. Open July-August 1999.
Battlesteads Hotel, Wark on Tyne (01434) 230209
The Old Rectory, Wark on Tyne (01434) 230223
Lyndale Guest House, Bellingham (01434) 220361(Tel &fax). ££££-PL-DR-LAU-SEC. Evening meal available. Also self-catering cottage.
The Cheviot Hotel, Main Street, Bellingham (01434) 220696. ££££-PL-DR-SEC-WKSH. Bar & restaurant menus also available.
The Black Bull Hotel, The Main, Bellingham (01434) 220226
Crofters End, The Croft, Bellingham (01434) 220034
CONTINUED ON PAGE 33

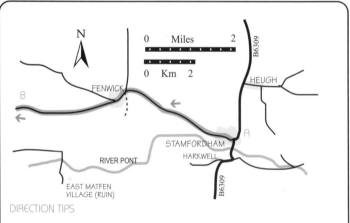

DIRECTION TIPS

A - B Follow the road across Stamfordham village green and out of the village, keeping the Bay Horse Inn on your L. Stay on this road through Fenwick (link route from Corbridge joins here from the L).

STAMFORDHAM - BELLINGHAM

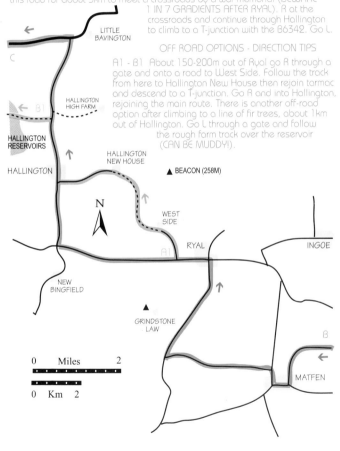

DIRECTION TIPS

B - C About 3km after Fenwick you enter the beautiful Matfen. In Matfen take the first R signed for Ryal, Ingoe and Capheaton. In 100-150m take the next L but beware of quarry traffic on this road. At the next T-junction go R, then pass Grindstone Law on the L. Enter Ryal and at the crossroads go L. Continue on this road for about 3km to meet a crossroads by a war memorial (BEWARE 1 IN 7 GRADIENTS AFTER RYAL). R at the crossroads and continue through Hallington to climb to a T-junction with the B6342. Go L.

OFF ROAD OPTIONS - DIRECTION TIPS

A1 - B1 About 150-200m out of Ryal go R through a gate and onto a road to West Side. Follow the track from here to Hallington New House then rejoin tarmac and descend to a T-junction. Go R and into Hallington, rejoining the main route. There is another off-road option after climbing to a line of fir trees, about 1km out of Hallington. Go L through a gate and follow the rough farm track over the reservoir (CAN BE MUDDY!).

DIRECTION TIPS

C - D Take the first R off the B6342, signed for Throckrington, just past the Dove Cot ruin up on your L. Pass through this lonely hamlet and onto a gated road. At the next T-junction go R, signed for Carrycoats. * Pass over the end of Colt Crag reservoir and L at the next T-junction, signed for Birtley and Wark. L at the next fork, for Corbridge and Wark and come to the A68. Go L then immediate R, signed Birtley and Wark.

OFF-ROAD OPTION - DIRECTION TIPS

B1 - C1 After crossing over Hallington Reservoirs simply stay on the track in a straight line to cross the B6342 and into Little Swinburne. Head R here and where a road joins from the R pick up the directions above at the * mark.

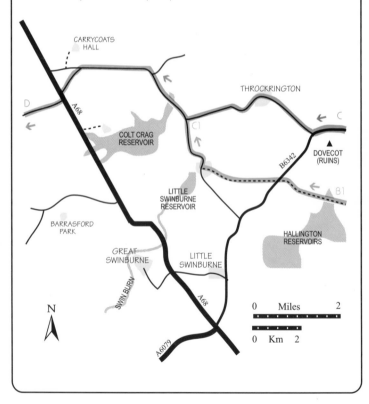

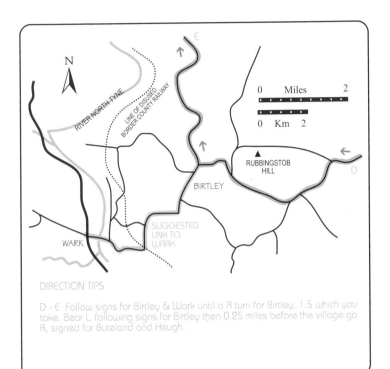

DIRECTION TIPS

D - E Follow signs for Birtley & Wark until a R turn for Birtley, 1.5 which you take. Bear L, following signs for Birtley then 0.25 miles before the village go R, signed for Buteland and Heugh.

STAMFORDHAM TO BELLINGHAM - ACCOMMODATION - CONTINUED

Lynn View, Bellingham (01434) 220344
Riverdale Hall Hotel, Riverdale, Bellingham (01434) 220254
Rose & Crown Hotel, Manchester Square, Bellingham (01434) 220202
Westfield House, Bellingham (01434) 220340
Bellingham Youth Hostel, Woodburn Road (01434) 220313. £-DR-SEC.
    Demesne Farm, Bellingham (01434) 220258. Brown Rigg Caravan Park, Bellingham (01434) 220175.

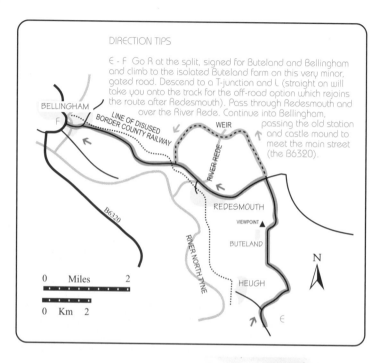

DIRECTION TIPS

E - F Go R at the split, signed for Buteland and Bellingham and climb to the isolated Buteland farm on this very minor, gated road. Descend to a T-junction and L (straight on will take you onto the track for the off-road option which rejoins the route after Redesmouth). Pass through Redesmouth and over the River Rede. Continue into Bellingham, passing the old station and castle mound to meet the main street (the B6320).

BELLINGHAM
F
LINE OF DISUSED
BORDER COUNTY RAILWAY
WEIR
RIVER REDE
B6320
REDESMOUTH
VIEWPOINT
BUTELAND
RIVER NORTH TYNE
N
HEUGH
E

0   Miles   2

0   Km   2

Disused Border Counties Line over Tarset Burn (section 3)

Bellingham Town Hall with the 'Boxer' gun (section 2/3)

3 BELLINGHAM - KIELDER

Section Distance 20 miles / 32km

Off-road 9 miles / 14.5 km with an option to do the whole section on metalled roads

The Route Quiet minor roads lead through the upper reaches of the North Tyne Valley to Falstone and then Kielder Reservoir. From here you have several possible options; the road along the southern shore of Kielder Reservoir can be busy, whilst the gradients on the forestry roads of the northern shore aren't too challenging. If you want to slow the pace and reduce the distance you have to cycle you can incorporate a trip on the Kielder Water ferry as part of the route (seasonal opening - Easter to October, 4 times daily, stopping at Tower Knowe and Leaplish). You might also want to take the OS maps for both this and the next section, as substantial parts of them are through thick coniferous forest. Careful navigation is needed as a thick wall of trees will often obscure any landmark. A compass is also advised.

BELLINGHAM TO KIELDER

• In the upper reaches of the **North Tyne Valley** there seems even less settlement than further down the valley; this area was once a bone of Anglo-Scottish contention where war, looting and pillaging was rife. It was not until the nineteenth century that most former wasteland with any potential had been converted into cultivable land. Perhaps this late settlement is one reason for the lack of villages, even today.

• **Tarset Castle** near Lanehead now lies in grass-covered ruins. Once garrisoned by the English it was burnt down by the local Charlton family, probably because it was interfering with their Reiving!

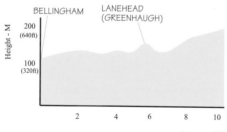

• **Falstone** Secluded hamlet on a tributary of the North Tyne where the Northumberland National Park and the Border Forest Park meet. The farmhouse next to the church incorporates the remains of a fortified house. Cafe / information point and village shop. **Blackcock Inn** Meals 11-2 and 7-9 (all day in summer). Various real ales and Beamish.

• **Stannersburn** Small village just south of the route, huddled around the **Pheasant Inn**. Meals 12-2.30 & 7-9. Theakstons, Timothy Taylors and Marstons.

• **Kielder Water** is vast; in fact it's the largest man-made lake in western Europe. The Reivers option along the southern shore takes you past **Tower Knowe Visitor Centre** and **Leaplish Waterside Park**, with the chance to have a go at numerous water sports. (01434) 250312. Completed in the 80s, the reservoir has two dams, Falstone and Bakethin, the latter being used to control water supply into Kielder. A superb railway viaduct carries a disused railway line across the northern end of the huge expanse of water. It was once part of the Border Counties Railway, designed to carry coal from Hexham up the North Tyne Valley to Riccarton Junction in Scotland. **Water cruises** are available in season. (01434) 240398. The ferry goes between Leaplish Waterside Park and the north shore (limited number of cycles allowed on). ⚲ **Leaplish Barn Cycling Centre** (cycle hire) (01434) 250312.

• **Kielder** village is a product of the forestry development in this area in the 1950s, most of the workaday houses being designed for forestry workers. Small village shop. The quarter of a million acres of dense trees provide pulp for paper, fencing and board. **Anglers Arms** Meals 11am-10pm (winter noon-10pm). Snacks & bar meals. ⚲ **Kielder Bikes**, Castle Hill (cycle hire centre), also at Hawkhope car park. Spares, repairs & rescue service (01434) 250392.

• The **Kielder Castle Visitor Centre** gives information on the walking and cycling possibilities in the 60,000 hectares of forest that are on Kielder's doorstep and is housed in what was originally a gothic eighteenth century shooting lodge. It also has a cafe. (01434) 250209.

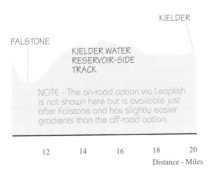

KIELDER

FALSTONE

KIELDER WATER
RESERVOIR-SIDE
TRACK

NOTE - The on-road option via Leaplish is not shown here but is available just after Falstone and has slightly easier gradients than the off-road option.

12   14   16   18   20

Distance - Miles

BELLINGHAM TO KIELDER - ACCOMMODATION

Ivy Cottage, Lanehead, Tarset (01434) 240337. £££-PL-DR-LAU-SEC.
Hollybush Inn, Greenhaugh (01434) 240391
High Yarrow Farm, Falstone (01434) 240264. Open 1st April-31st October. £££-PL-DR-SEC.
Ridge End Farm, Falstone (01434) 240395. £££-PL-DR-LAU-SEC-Basic tools.
Blackcock Inn, Falstone (01434) 240200. ££££-PL-DR-LAU-SEC-Basic tools. Directly on the route.
Braefoot, Falstone (01434) 240238
Falstone Village Hall (01434) 240296 (Basic facilities only)
Woodside, Low Yarrow, Falstone (01434) 240443
Spring Cottage, Stannersburn (01434) 240388. £££(£)-PL-DR-LAU-SEC.
Pheasant Inn, Stannersburn (01434) 240382. £££££-PL-DR-LAU-SEC.
Gowanburn, en route on northern shore near Kielder village. (01434) 250254. £££-PL-DR-SEC. March to December only.
Deadwater Farm, nr Kielder (01434) 250216
⚠ **Kielder Caravan Club Site**, Leaplish (01434) 250278. **Forestry Commission Caravan & Camp Site**, Kielder (01434) 250291. **Leaplish Waterside Campsite**, Kielder Water (01434) 250312.

North Tyne Valley landscape (section 3)

Drinking fountain in Falstone (section 3)

BELLINGHAM - KIELDER

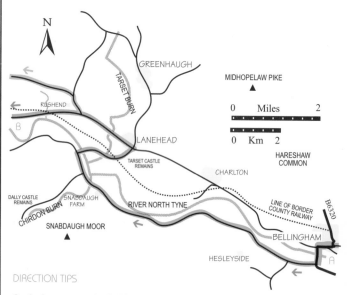

N

GREENHAUGH

MIDHOPELAW PIKE ▲

TARSET BURN

RUSHEND

B

LANEHEAD

0   Miles   2

0   Km   2

HARESHAW COMMON

TARSET CASTLE REMAINS

CHARLTON

DALLY CASTLE REMAINS

SNABDAUGH FARM

RIVER NORTH TYNE

LINE OF BORDER COUNTY RAILWAY

B6320

CHIRDON BURN

SNABDAUGH MOOR ▲

BELLINGHAM

HESLEYSIDE

A

DIRECTION TIPS

A - B On meeting the B6320 in the centre of Bellingham go L along the main street, signed for Wark and Hexham. Follow the road past the Town Hall on the L and bend out of Bellingham. About 50-100m after crossing over the North Tyne river go R and enter the Northumberland National Park. Follow this beautiful road alongside the river for about 7km to come to a T-junction. Go R to immediately cross the North Tyne again. Climb steeply into the village of Lanehead and take the first L , opposite the church, signed for Donkleywood. Drop steeply to cross Tarset Burn again. At the first split over the burn bear L and continue on the gated road. The off-road option is up to the R at this first split. If following it keep L on the tarmac which then becomes a rough track.

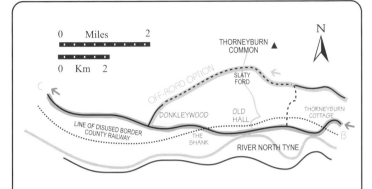

DIRECTION TIPS

▲ STOKOE HIGH CRAGS

B - C Continue on the road, over the line of the old railway at Thorneyburn Cottage and through Old Hall to climb to Donkleywood, both no more than clusters of houses and farms. (If on the off-road option you will join just after Donkleywood on the road marked unfit for motor vehicles). Just before Donkleywood you cross over the old railway line on a bridge. After passing through Donkleywood simply follow your nose on this minor road and into Falstone.

Kielder Reservoir (section 4)

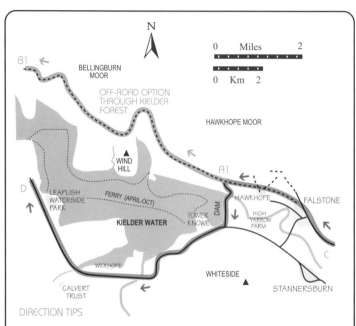

DIRECTION TIPS

C - D Coming into Falstone take the R turn, just before a stone bridge, marked as a cul-de-sac. After 30-40m take the first L split, down a track marked 'no lorry access'. At the next T-junction go L then head straight over the crossroads at the farm building of Hawkhope. Climb to the end of Kielder Dam, by Hawkhope car park. For the road option head L, across the dam itself, then R onto the road along the southern side of Kielder Reservoir NOTE -THIS ROAD IS FAST & BUSY IN SEASON.

OFF-ROAD OPTION ALONG THE NORTHERN SHORE

A1 - B1 Do not bear L at the corner of Kielder Dam but carry straight on, along the forestry track. Simply follow signs for the Reivers route.
If you can't find these then simply follow the red arrow number 6 signs. These show the round reservoir route, which is the same as the Reivers as far as Kielder village.

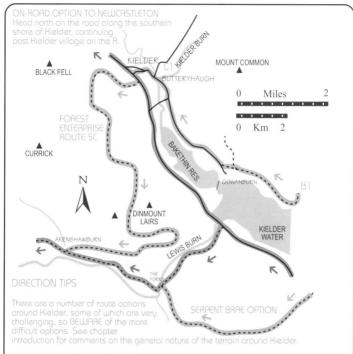

ON-ROAD OPTION TO NEWCASTLETON
Head north on the road along the southern shore of Kielder, continuing past Kielder village on the R.

▲ BLACK FELL

KIELDER

KIELDER BURN

BUTTERYHAUGH

MOUNT COMMON ▲

FOREST ENTERPRISE ROUTE 5C

▲ CURRICK

BAKETHIN RES

GOWANBURN

B1

N

▲ DINMOUNT LAIRS

KIELDER WATER

AKENSHAWBURN

LEWIS BURN

THE FORKS

DIRECTION TIPS

There are a number of route options around Kielder, some of which are very challenging, so BEWARE of the more difficult options. See chapter introduction for comments on the general nature of the terrain around Kielder.

SERPENT BRAE OPTION

OPTIONS FROM LEAPLISH WATERSIDE PARK, SOUTH SHORE ROAD
1. VIA LEWIS BURN Continue on the road along the southern shore until, about 3km after passing Leaplish, you see the turning signed for the picnic area up Lewis Burn. Go L up here and you are now on the off-road option to Newcastleton.
2. SERPENT BRAE Pick up this option at Leaplish Waterside Park. Follow signs under the underpass and up a steep difficult section to a track T-junction. Go R here and follow the main track until heading down a signed break in trees on the R. Follow signs through very difficult pine forest to emerge at the track by The Forks.
ALONG THE NORTHERN SHORE
B1 - C1 Continue to follow Reivers route / red arrow no.6 signs along the northern shore on good forestry tracks. About 8km after passing the NE corner of the reservoir meet a tarmac road above Gowanburn and go R. Continue on this road to the T-junction by Butteryhaugh Bridge and R to pass through Butteryhaugh. Cross over Kielder Burn and L at the T-junction (Kielder Castle up to the R). Pass the Anglers Arms on the R and follow this road to a T-junction with the main southern shore road. L onto the road. There are two options from here.
1. Follow signs R onto forestry ride 5c. This is a very difficult option with EXTENDED CLIMBS. Follow Reivers signs to rejoin the main route at Akenshaw Burn and R.
2. The easier option is to follow the road for about 3.5km then go R, following signs for Lewis Burn and onto the off-road option to Newcastleton.

4 KIELDER - BEWCASTLE

Section Distance 29 miles / 47km
with a shorter 20 mile / 32km option
avoiding Kielder via Leaplish and missing
out Newcastleton.

Off-road 13.5 miles / 22km

The Route This is a section of two contrasting parts; initially come the dense forests of Kielder, Kershope and Newcastleton, followed by the open and lonely Bewcastle Fells. The borders area is extremely sparsely populated and provides an ideal habitat for numerous deer. The lack of population centres means accommodation may be in short supply so it's wise to book in advance for this section; Newcastleton is the main settlement and if you are bypassing this you should know where you are staying at the earliest possible stage. Be prepared for some challenging gradients on this relatively long section, especially if you opt to take the off-road option to Newcastleton, which crosses the very steep-sided Tweeden Burn. To decide which option to take from Kielder to Newcastleton see page 43 in the previous chapter. WARNING Between Kielder and Newcastleton there are no services so go well prepared with food and adequate clothing. The longer and more off-road your choice of route is the more vital this becomes!

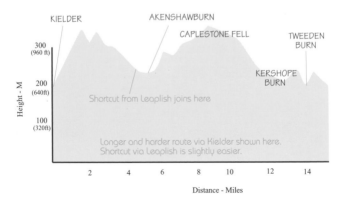

KIELDER TO BEWCASTLE

• The massive **forestry developments** between Kielder and Newcastleton are relatively recent. Although you now use good quality forestry tracks, some of these follow the lines of old toll roads developed to exploit the **local coal industry**, centred around Lewis Burn in centuries past. In fact there was once a Toll House at Akenshaw. There were plans for a cross border mail-coach route to take traffic from London, complete with inn, but this never happened.

• **Newcastleton** lies just within Scotland, in the heart of lonely Liddesdale. **Liddesdale Heritage Centre** shows the history of the valley and its people and has a unique bicentennial tapestry. Open Easter - September. Small admission charge. The town was planned and built by the local landowner in the eighteenth century. Douglas Square remains the centre for events such as the Traditional Music Festival in July.

• At Kershopefoot near **Kershope Bridge** Wardens of the Marches used to judge on international disputes.

• The magnificent approach to **Bewcastle** reveals a most unusual hamlet, looking rather exposed in a broad sweep of wild moorland. A cluster of residences, farms and a church are grouped around crumbling castle ruins. The **castle** is probably based on an earlier Roman fort, effectively an early warning station for Hadrian's Wall. The Roman fort seems to have been built over an even earlier shrine to a native war god. The present ruins are probably Norman. The **cross** next to the church is Anglo-Saxon and around thirteen hundred years old! The runic inscriptions bear the name of Alcfrith, a sub-king of Northumbria. The **Past & Present** exhibition is housed in the small building in the churchyard and is open 10-8 daily. Interpretive panels give a history of the settlement plus archaeological finds and a mural. The **Lime Kiln Inn** is in Shopford, just south of the church and castle.

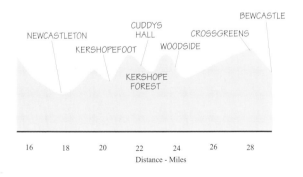

KIELDER TO BEWCASTLE - ACCOMMODATION

12 Whitchester Lane, Newcastleton (013873) 75826. ££-PL-DR-LAU-SEC.
Hillus, The Wood, Newcastleton (013873) 75434
Newlands Country Guest House, Newcastleton (013873) 76264
Borders Honey Farm, Newcastleton (013873) 76737
10a Douglas Square, Newcastleton (013873) 75257
1 Mid Liddel Street, Newcastleton (013873) 75387
Woodside, North Hermitage Street, Newcastleton (013873) 75431
Liddesdale Hotel, Douglas Square, Newcastleton (013873) 75434
The Grapes Hotel, Douglas Square, Newcastleton (013873) 75245
Bailey Mill about 9 miles south-east of Newcastleton (016977) 48617. ££(£)-PL-DR-LAU-SEC-WKSH. Additional features include jacuzzi, steam shower and pressure hose for cleaning bikes. All meals available. Possible choice of B&B and self-catering apartments. Near the route.
⚊ **Lidalia Caravan Park**, Newcastleton (013873) 75819

Bikers at Kielder Forest (section 4)

The single width track down to Kershope Burn (section 4)

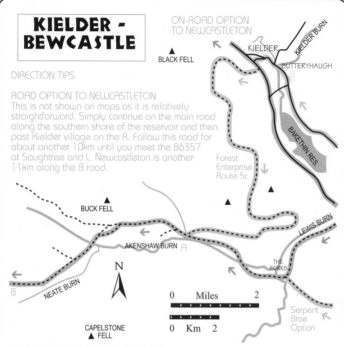

KIELDER - BEWCASTLE

ON-ROAD OPTION TO NEWCASTLETON

▲ BLACK FELL

KIELDER

KIELDER BURN

BUTTERYHAUGH

BAKETHIN RES.

DIRECTION TIPS

ROAD OPTION TO NEWCASTLETON

This is not shown on maps as it is relatively straightforward. Simply continue on the main road along the southern shore of the reservoir and then past Kielder village on the R. Follow this road for about another 10km until you meet the B6357 at Saughtree and L. Newcastleton is another 11km along the B road.

Forest Enterprise Route 5c

▲ BUCK FELL

▲

▲

LEWIS BURN

AKENSHAW BURN ᴀ

THE FORKS

N

NEATE BURN

ʙ

| 0 | Miles | 2 |

Serpent Brae Option

CAPELSTONE ▲ FELL

| 0 | Km | 2 |

OFF-ROAD OPTION TO NEWCASTLETON

A - B For the various options on access onto Lewis Burn see page 43. (Unless you want a very difficult option it is recommended that you ascend Lewis Burn on the main track from the road, rather than joining from route 5c or Serpent Brae. Simply head up Lewis Burn and past the car park and picnic area). Cross over a bridge just after the group of buildings known as The Forks. (Serpent Brae option joins here). Shortly after this you cross over to the northern side of Lewis Burn (stream now on your L) and continue on the main forest track for about another 1.5km and past Akenshaw Cottages (strenuous alternative route from northern end of Kielder joins here on the R). At the first split after the cottages go L, signed for Scotch Knowe and Kershopefoot. Shortly join a T-junction with a good quality track and L. Descend over a bridge and carry on, on the main track. At the next split go L (R appears to head towards the mast on Larriston Fells).

WARNING - THE OFF-ROAD OPTION BETWEEN KIELDER AND NEWCASTLETON HAS NO SERVICES AND VIRTUALLY NO HOUSES. MAKE SURE YOU HAVE ENOUGH FOOD, DRINK AND SUFFICIENT WET WEATHER CLOTHING!

REIVERS LANDSCAPES
Above: Rolling green estate land next to the River North Tyne (section 3)
Below left: Cullercoats (alternative start option, section 1)
Below right: Bassenthwaite village (off-road option, section 7)

Above: Dramatic Lakeland landscape near Bassenthwaite (off-road option, section 7)
Below: Falstone village, approaching Kielder Reservoir (section 3)

Above: Looking down over Kielder Water (section 3)
Below: The River Eden, on The Reivers just out of Carlisle (section 6)

REIVERS BIKERS

Above: Near Kershope Burn (section 4)
Below left: Easy cycling on Kielder Forest tracks (section 3)
Below right: The Kielder ferry provides a restful route option (section 3)

Above: Bridleway by the old spoil heap, near Burradon (section 1)
Below: Cyclists near the start of the route at Tynemouth (section 1)

REIVERS TRACKS

Above: Scenic green track by the River Caldew, near Dalston (off-road option, section 6)
Below: Bike's-eye view of the good quality tracks at Kielder Forest (section 3)
Opposite: Take a break! A good picnic spot above the River Eden path (section 6)

CARLISLE'S GRANDEUR

Above: Carlisle Castle (section 5)
Below: The Citadel, gateway to Carlisle (section 5)

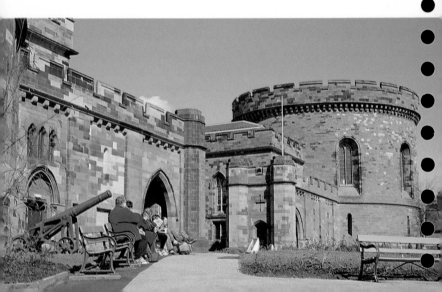

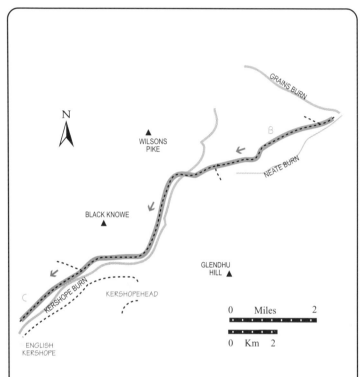

DIRECTION TIPS

B - C At the next split in the track leave the better quality track and head R
down a lighter coloured vehicle track. This gradually narrows towards
Kershope Burn. WARNING Just before Kershope Burn watch out for the steep
rocky descent. Bend R over the small bridge and then L, to follow the course
of the small, pretty stream on your L (you are now just inside the Scottish
border - the stream is in fact the border at this point). Ignore the first track
that leads off up to the R.

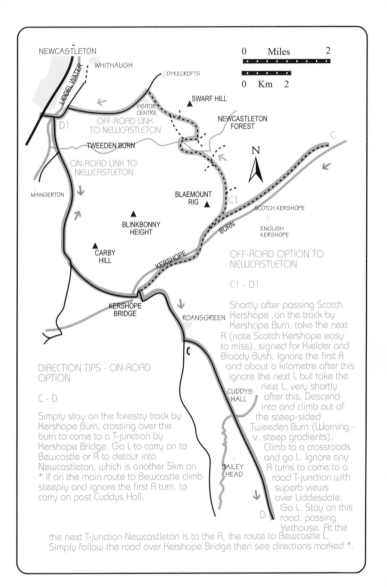

NEWCASTLETON

WHITHAUGH

DYKECROFTS

LIDDEL WATER

VISITOR CENTRE

SWARF HILL

NEWCASTLETON FOREST

OFF-ROAD LINK TO NEWCASTLETON

D1

TWEEDEN BURN

ON-ROAD LINK TO NEWCASTLETON

N

MANGERTON

BLAEMOUNT RIG

C1

SCOTCH KERSHOPE

BLINKBONNY HEIGHT

ENGLISH KERSHOPE

BURN

CARBY HILL

KERSHOPE

OFF-ROAD OPTION TO NEWCASTLETON

C1 - D1

KERSHOPE BRIDGE

ROANSGREEN

Shortly after passing Scotch Kershope, on the track by Kershope Burn, take the next R (note Scotch Kershope easy to miss), signed for Kielder and Bloody Bush. Ignore the first R and about a kilometre after this ignore the next L but take the next L, very shortly after this. Descend into and climb out of the steep-sided Tweeden Burn (Warning - v. steep gradients). Climb to a crossroads and go L. Ignore any R turns to come to a road T-junction with superb views over Liddesdale. Go L. Stay on this road, passing Yethouse. At the

CUDDYS HALL

BAILEY HEAD

DIRECTION TIPS - ON-ROAD OPTION

C - D

Simply stay on the forestry track by Kershope Burn, crossing over the burn to come to a T-junction by Kershope Bridge. Go L to carry on to Bewcastle or R to detour into Newcastleton, which is another 5km on. * If on the main route to Bewcastle climb steeply and ignore the first R turn, to carry on past Cuddys Hall.

D

the next T-junction Newcastleton is to the R, the route to Bewcastle L. Simply follow the road over Kershope Bridge then see directions marked *.

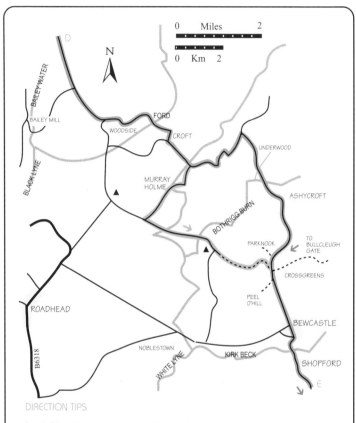

DIRECTION TIPS

D - E After Cuddys Hall ignore the next R turn unless using the popular accommodation facilities at Bailey Mill. Descend and bend L through the farming settlement of Woodside then through a ford. Bend L in front of The Croft and at the next T-junction the on-road route is to the L (R takes you on the OFF-ROAD OPTION. To follow this bear L at the next junction to a ford with footbridge. Over another ford follow the road in a straight line, leaving the tarmac onto a track. At the next junction go R to rejoin the main route). R at the next unsigned junction and over two streams in quick succession. Cross over the byroad where the off-road option joins, and stay on this road into Bewcastle.

The Bewcastle Cross (section 4/5)

Using the cycle ramp by the River Eden (section 6)

5 BEWCASTLE - CARLISLE

Section Distance 27 miles / 43.5km   **Off-road** All on quiet minor roads

The Route Gradually the Bewcastle Fells are left behind and an easy long descent onto the Solway Plain follows, the lie of the land flattening as you get nearer to Carlisle. There are superb views over the broad River Eden around Rockliffe and Stainton before your arrival in Cumbria's major city, Carlisle, with its historic sights and distinctive architecture. If you want to visit Longtown it's about 5km north of the main route and there is a decent off-road link.

BEWCASTLE TO CARLISLE

• **Askerton** A tiny farming hamlet grouped around a small, still-inhabited castle. First built as a fortified house in the 15th century, towers were added in the time of Elizabeth I. Once the home of infamous Warden of the Marches, Belted Will.
• **Kirkcambeck** is clustered around a church. The village grew up around an 11th century church but this was destroyed by the Scots and now only an old archway remains in front of the new church.
• Around **Hethersgill** peat extraction is one of the predominant industries. **Pointer Dog Inn** Meals 12-9pm. Boddingtons and Worthingtons.
• **Longtown** Border town established in the 18th century by the Grahams; before this the area was seen as too violent for permanent settlement. Being Reiving country the Grahams felt compelled to build numerous pele towers where families and livestock were kept safe from raiders. The broad main street leads to a bridge over the beautiful Esk. Midland and Barclays banks on the main street, both with cashpoints. **Information** in the Community Centre at the south end of town (01228) 791876. Seasonal opening.

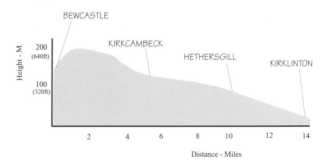

• **Westlinton** has a handy cafe.
• The quiet that now pervades **Rockliffe** belies the fact it was once a major shipbuilding centre, being just a few miles upstream of the Solway Firth. The main reminder now is the ship weathervane on the church. Its location remains impressive, perched on red cliffs above extensive tidal mudflats. **Crown and Thistle** pub does meals.

BEWCASTLE TO CARLISLE - ACCOMMODATION

Cracrop Farm, Kirkcambeck (016977) 48245. ££££-PL-DR-LAU-SEC-WKSH.
New Pallyards, Hethersgill (01228) 577308. ££££-PL-DR-LAU-SEC. B&B / self-catering. Dinner and supper available.
Lynebank House, Westlinton (01228) 792820
Briar Lee House, Longtown (01228) 791538
Metal Bridge House, Metal Bridge, Rockliffe (01228) 674695. £££-DR-SEC-Some tools.
⚠ **Oakbank Lakes Country Park**, Longtown (01228) 791108

Entering Carlisle (section 5)

WESTLINTON   ROCKLIFFE   CARLISLE

16   18   20   22   24   26
Distance - Miles

CARLISLE - HISTORY AND ATTRACTIONS

The grand city you see today has come to prosper despite its history at the centre of Border wars and a parliamentarian siege. Modern peace has seen it become the commercial, communications and administrative centre of Cumbria. The numbered attractions on the map opposite are described below:

1 **Carlisle Castle** First built in wood by Norman king William Rufus then later developed into this impressive stone structure. It's possible that 12th century additions were made by the Scots who captured the castle in 1135. It was captured and rebuilt several times after this. Look out for the 14th and 15th century wallcarvings. The keep is now a museum of the history of the Border Regiment. Open daily (English Heritage). Admission charge. (01228) 591922.

2 **Tullie House Museum** Impressive collections of Roman and prehistoric antiquities, porcelain and toys plus a gallery of 19th and 20th century British painting and a wildlife dome. Open all year. Admission charge. (01228) 534781.

3 **Carlisle Cathedral** This beautiful red sandstone building is one of the smallest cathedrals in England. Started life as the church of an Augustinian priory on the site. Beautiful stained glass from 14th to 20th centuries and Brougham Triptych altarpiece. Open all year. Free admission. (01228) 548151.

4 **Guildhall Museum** Housed in a brick and timber building dating from the 15th century. Home to such medieval guilds as the cordwainers, glovers and skinners, whose work is recreated here. Open Easter-Sept. Small admission charge. (01228) 534781.

5 **Victorian Covered Market**

6 **St Cuthbert's Church** Dates from the 18th century. Unique movable pulpit. Stained glass window tells the life of St. Cuthbert. Open all year. Free admission. Nearby is the **Tithe Barn** which sometimes has coffee mornings.

7 **Citadel and West Walls** Protected the southern approaches to the city (the castle protecting the northern ones). The Citadel was built in the 16th century and reconstructed in the 19th. The last shooting from this gate was by the Scots in 1745, trying to stop the advance of the Duke of Cumberland.

8 **Carlisle Railway Station** Superb Victorian facade, built in 1847. Between 1875 and 1922 seven railway companies operated services into Carlisle.

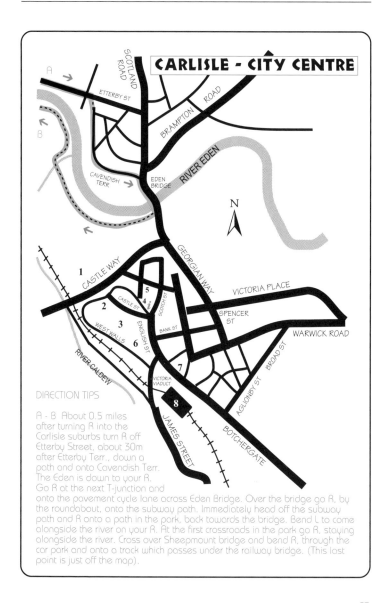

CARLISLE - CITY CENTRE

DIRECTION TIPS

A · B About 0.5 miles
after turning R into the
Carlisle suburbs turn R off
Etterby Street, about 30m
after Etterby Terr., down a
path and onto Cavendish Terr.
The Eden is down to your R.
Go R at the next T-junction and
onto the pavement cycle lane across Eden Bridge. Over the bridge go R, by
the roundabout, onto the subway path. Immediately head off the subway
path and R onto a path in the park, back towards the bridge. Bend L to come
alongside the river on your R. At the first crossroads in the park go R, staying
alongside the river. Cross over Sheepmount bridge and bend R, through the
car park and onto a track which passes under the railway bridge. (This last
point is just off the map).

CARLISLE - ACCOMMODATION

Fern Lee Guest House, 9 St Aidans Rd.Tel & fax (01228) 511930. £££-PL-DR-SEC. Evening meal available (booking necessary).
Craighead, 1 Hartington Place (01228) 596767. £££-DR-SEC.
Whitelea, 191 Warwick Road (01228) 533139. £££-PL-DR-SEC. Dinner available.
Howard Lodge, 90 Warwick Road (01228) 529842. £££(£)-DR-LAU-SEC-basic tools.
31 Howard Place (01228) 597080. £££££-PL-DR-LAU-SEC-Some tools. 1st March - 31st October.
Cumbria College of Art & Design, Brampton Road, Carlisle (01228) 400300 or (0468) 034576. £££-PL-DR-LAU-SEC. **Mid-July to mid-September only.**
Aaron House, 135 Warwick Road (01228) 536728
Abbey Court, 24 London Road (01228) 528696
Acer House, 146 Warwick Road (01228) 531562
Aidan View, 146 Warwick Road (01228) (01228) 532353
Chatsworth Guest House, 22 Chatsworth Square
Corner House, 87 Petteril Street (01228) 541942
Howard House, 27 Howard Place (01228) 01228) 529159
Marchmain, 151 Warwick Road (01228) 529551
Villa Soriso, 71 Scotland Road (01228) 533375
Riverston, 68 St James Road (01228) 818060

CARLISLE - OTHER INFORMATION

Tourist Information Old Town Hall, Greenmarket (01228) 625600
Hospital A&E at Cumberland Infirmary, Newtown Road (01228) 523444
Banks All major banks and Link outlets, with cashpoints, on or near the central pedestrianised area of English Street
♿ **Palace Cycle Stores**, 122 Botchergate (01228) 523142. **Scotby Cycles**, Bridge Street (01228) 546931.

Tullie House, Carlisle (section 5)

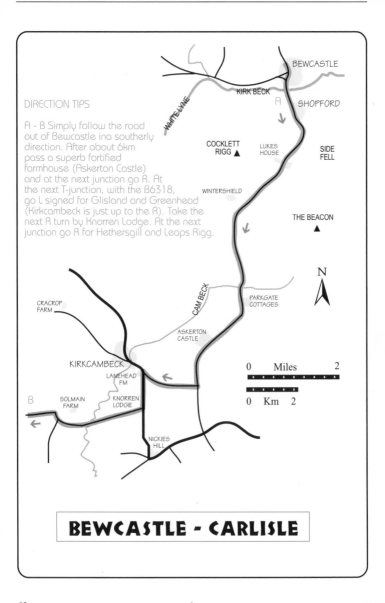

DIRECTION TIPS

A - B Simply follow the road
out of Bewcastle in a southerly
direction. After about 6km
pass a superb fortified
farmhouse (Askerton Castle)
and at the next junction go R. At
the next T-junction, with the B6318,
go L signed for Glisland and Greenhead
(Kirkcambeck is just up to the R). Take the
next R turn by Knorren Lodge. At the next
junction go R for Hethersgill and Leaps Rigg.

BEWCASTLE - CARLISLE

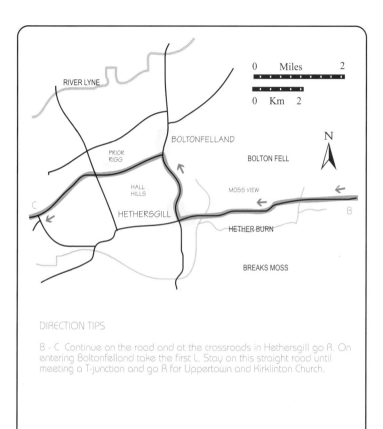

DIRECTION TIPS

B - C Continue on the road and at the crossroads in Hethersgill go R. On entering Boltonfelland take the first L. Stay on this straight road until meeting a T-junction and go R for Uppertown and Kirklinton Church.

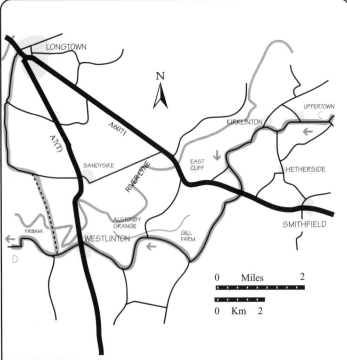

DIRECTION TIPS

C - D Turn L in Uppertown and at the next T-junction go R towards Kirklinton and Longtown. Very shortly come to another T-junction by the church in Kirklinton and L. Come to a crossroads with the A6071 and straight across. Take the first R (easy to miss - unsigned, under a line of pylons). At the next T-junction go L for Blackford and Carlisle. Take the next R and come to a crossroads with the A7 in the village of Westlinton. Head straight over the crossroads and out of the village. (The off-road link to Longtown is on your R immediately on leaving the last house in Westlinton).

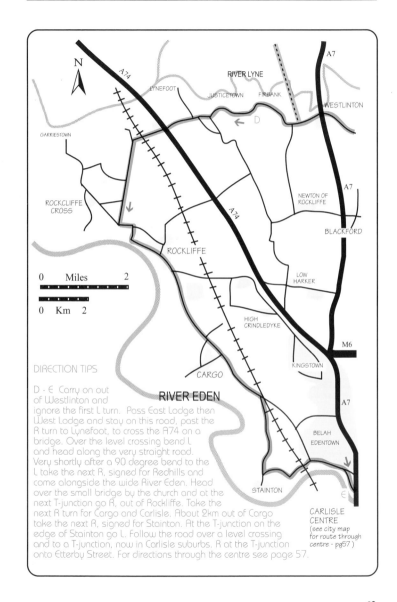

N

A74

RIVER LYNE

LYNEFOOT

JUSTICETOWN   FIRBANK

A7

WESTLINTON

D

GARRIESTOWN

NEWTON OF
ROCKLIFFE

A7

ROCKCLIFFE
CROSS

A74

BLACKFORD

ROCKLIFFE

LOW
HARKER

0   Miles   2

0   Km   2

HIGH
CRINDLEDYKE

M6

DIRECTION TIPS

KINGSTOWN

CARGO

RIVER EDEN

A7

D - E Carry on out
of Westlinton and
ignore the first L turn. Pass East Lodge then
West Lodge and stay on this road, past the
R turn to Lynefoot, to cross the A74 on a
bridge. Over the level crossing bend L
and head along the very straight road.
Very shortly after a 90 degree bend to the
L take the next R, signed for Redhills and
come alongside the wide River Eden. Head
over the small bridge by the church and at the
next T-junction go R, out of Rockliffe. Take the
next R turn for Cargo and Carlisle. About 2km out of Cargo
take the next R, signed for Stainton. At the T-junction on the
edge of Stainton go L. Follow the road over a level crossing
and to a T-junction, now in Carlisle suburbs. R at the T-junction
onto Etterby Street. For directions through the centre see page 57.

BELAH
EDENTOWN

STAINTON

E

CARLISLE
CENTRE
(see city map
for route through
centre - pg57)

6 CARLISLE - HESKET
NEWMARKET

Section Distance 27 miles / 43.5km

Off-road About 7 miles. Also the possibility of completing the whole section on minor roads.

The Route After leaving Carlisle alongside the River Eden you find yourself passing through a series of quaint red brick villages near the flat Eden floodplain. Through Dalston you leave the easy pedalling behind and start the more serious climbing towards the edge of the Caldbeck Fells. The northern edge of the Lake District is a fairly remote area so, as near Kielder, make sure you have accommodation sorted and allow plenty of time to complete the route. The off-road options add significantly to the difficulty of the section but the tracks around Dalston and Raughtonhead are stunningly pretty.

CARLISLE TO HESKET NEWMARKET

• **Kirkandrews upon Eden** There is no church or 'kirk' as the name suggests, only a churchyard. A canal, then a railway, once passed through the village but the railway disappeared in the Beeching cuts in 1964.

• **Beaumont** St Mary's Church stands on a small mound which gives good views north over the Solway Firth, east towards Carlisle and south towards the start of the Lake District. As at Kirkandrews, Hadrian's Wall ran through the village.

• The **Edward I Monument** is found up a track to your right, about a mile before entering Burgh by Sands. It commemorates the death here of this warlike king, who died whilst on his way to do battle with the Scots.

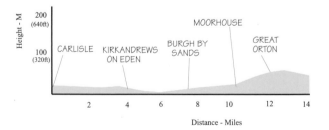

- **Burgh by Sands** The church tower here has slits from which arrows would have been fired to defend the villagers, harboured inside, against marauding Scots. There are a number of thatched houses here; at one time thatch was used on 'clay daubins', the original form of building from local clay and boulders. The **Greyhound** serves Greenalls.
- **Moorhouse** has the **Royal Oak.**
- **Great Orton** is home to the **Wellington Inn**, serving Hartleys.
- **Dalston** During the Industrial Revolution this village boasted four cotton mills and a flax mill. The heart of the village is the square which as well as the church has the **Bluebell Inn**, shop and cafe. A pele tower with turret stands beside the former Dalston Hall.
- **Rose Castle** is a magnificent orange-brown sandstone building amidst trees and was home to the Bishops of Carlisle for seven centuries.
- **Sebergham** and **Churchtown** once had more people than Penrith but today are little more than hamlets.
- **Hesket Newmarket** is centred around an open sided market building on the village green which has survived from the days of sheep and cattle trading, which stopped in the 19th century. **Old Crown pub**.
- **Caldbeck** is an alternative end to this section, about 2km from Hesket Newmarket and just off the route at the start of section 7. The 17th and 18th centuries saw the development of woollen, bobbin, paper and saw mills here. In the churchyard is the grave of the famous huntsman John Peel. The restored **Priests Mill** houses craft shops and a restaurant.

CARLISLE TO HESKET NEWMARKET - ACCOMMODATION

Cumbria Outdoor Centre, Fell Side (017687) 72816
Denton Guest House, Hesket Newmarket (016974) 78415. £££-PL-DR-SEC. Dinner available.

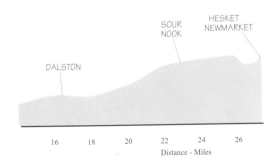

Newlands Grange, Hesket Newmarket (016974) 78676. Closed December. PL-DR-LAU-SEC-Basic tools.
The Briars, Friar Row, Caldbeck (016974) 78633. Open February to December. £££-PL-DR-LAU-SEC-Basic tools.
Parkend Restaurant & Country Hotel, Parkend, Caldbeck (016974) 78494. ££££-PL-DR-SEC. A la carte dinner also available.
  △ **Orton Grange**, nr Great Orton. Outdoor heated swimming pool and coffee shop (summer only). (01228) 710252. **Dalston Hall Caravan Park**, Dalston (01228) 710165.

The off-road option passes in front of Lime House School (section 6)

DIRECTION TIPS - FOR ROUTE THROUGH CENTRE SEE PAGE 57

A - B After passing under the railway bridge keep on the riverside path to pass under a disused railway viaduct. Immediately under this push your bike up the cycle ramp at the side of a set of steps. In the open area above the steps take the R-hand path and follow it as it bends L to emerge on an industrial estate at Thomas Lane. Go R and immediate L to the T-junction at the top of Marconi Road. R onto this FAST road - take care. Follow this road for about 3km and on entering Kirkandrews on Eden take the first R onto a quieter minor road. You may wish to carry straight on at this junction; this will bring you straight into Burgh by Sands and avoid the longer but quieter loop through Beaumont.

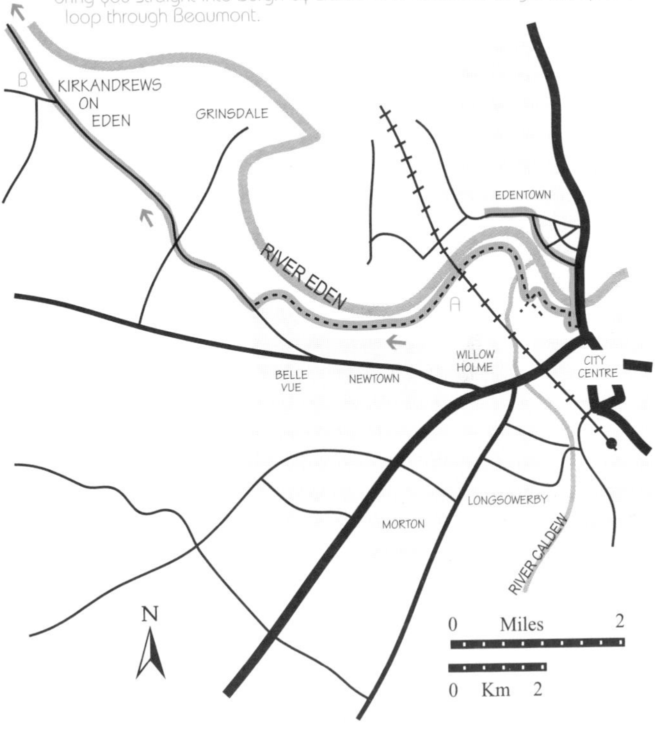

KIRKANDREWS ON EDEN

GRINSDALE

EDENTOWN

RIVER EDEN

WILLOW HOLME

CITY CENTRE

BELLE VUE

NEWTOWN

LONGSOWERBY

MORTON

RIVER CALDEW

N

| 0 | Miles | 2 |

| 0 | Km | 2 |

CARLISLE - HESKET NEWMARKET

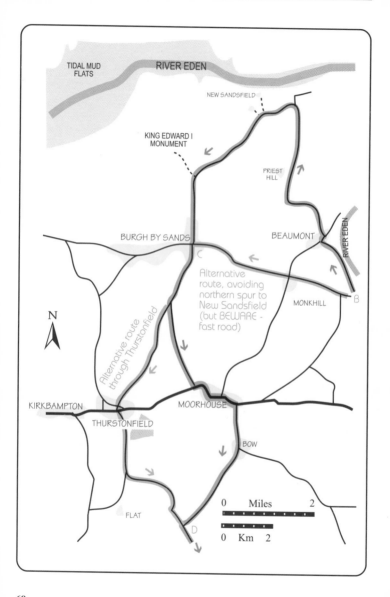

DIRECTION TIPS

B - C Out of Kirkandrews on Eden climb to a T-junction in the pretty village of Beaumont. Go R then first L in the village centre, signed for Burgh via Sandsfield. Simply follow this lonely minor road as it heads north to the edge of the Eden estuary and then turns back on itself and heads south to Burgh by Sands (about 5km between Beaumont and Burgh by Sands). Note the possible option of avoiding this spur on a busier road from Kirkandrews on Eden to Burgh by Sands (see previous map also).

C - D At the crossroads in Burgh by Sands go straight across and follow this road for just over 2km to a T-junction with the B5307 (note alternative route through Thurstonfield is on the R after about 1km - see map). L at the T-junction and into Moorhouse. On the edge of Moorhouse turn R, signed for Great Orton. Ignore the first minor L which goes to Little Orton. At the next T-junction go L.

Lakeland scenery (section 6)

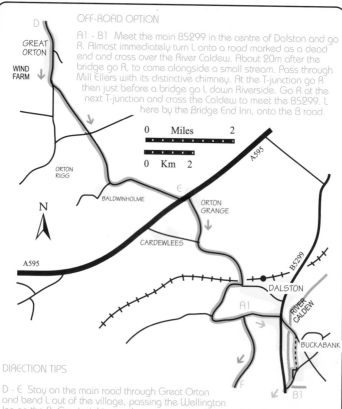

OFF-ROAD OPTION

A1 - B1 Meet the main B5299 in the centre of Dalston and go R. Almost immediately turn L onto a road marked as a dead end and cross over the River Caldew. About 20m after the bridge go R, to come alongside a small stream. Pass through Mill Ellers with its distinctive chimney. At the T-junction go R then just before a bridge go L down Riverside. Go R at the next T-junction and cross the Caldew to meet the B5299. L here by the Bridge End Inn, onto the B road.

DIRECTION TIPS

D - E Stay on the main road through Great Orton and bend L out of the village, passing the Wellington Inn on the R. Go straight over the next crossroads, signed for Baldwinholme and Dalston. Pass Baldwinholme on the R and come to the A595 (VERY BUSY AND FAST).

E - F Go L then immediate R at this difficult junction (pushing along the pavement is advisable) and pass Orton Grange camp site on the L. At the next T-junction go L (Dalston 1.25). Coming into Dalston's outskirts cross over the railway and go immediate R. After a stiff climb go L at the next T-junction. Coming into Dalston you must decide whether to opt for the on-road or off-road option. The on-road option is R coming into Dalston, signed Gill. For the off-road option carry straight on and follow the off-road directions above.

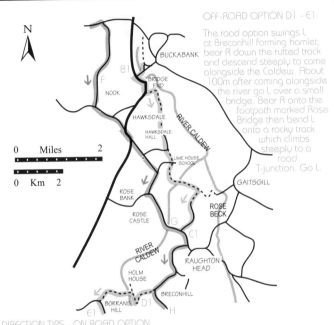

N

OFF-ROAD OPTION D1 - E1

The road option swings L at Breconhill farming hamlet; bear R down the rutted track and descend steeply to come alongside the Caldew. About 100m after coming alongside the river go L over a small bridge. Bear R onto the footpath marked Rose Bridge then bend L onto a rocky track which climbs steeply to a road T-junction. Go L.

BUCKABANK

B1

F

NOOK

BRIDGE END

HAWKSDALE

HAWKSDALE HALL

RIVER CALDEW

LIME HOUSE SCHOOL

GAITSGILL

ROSE BANK

ROSE CASTLE

ROSE BECK

G

C1

RIVER CALDEW

RAUGHTON HEAD

HOLM HOUSE

BORRANS HILL

BRECONHILL

D1

E1

H

0   Miles   2

0   Km   2

DIRECTION TIPS - ON ROAD OPTION

F - G Just under 2km out of Dalston come to a T-junction and go L, signed Raughton Head and Welton. Carry on to a T-junction with the B5299 and R signed Welton and Caldbeck. Take the next L in about 100m and stay on this road to descend over the Caldew at Rose Bridge.

G - H Pass the turning for Raughtonhead Hill where the off-road option joins on the L. Coming into Raughton Head turn R opposite the church. Stay on this road past Breconhill Farm (off road option D1-E1 R here).

OFF-ROAD OPTION B1 - C1

Climb away from Bridge End on the B5299. Before leaving Bridge End look out for a tarmac track on the L, between Little Pinch and Sudale (right of way). Follow the track into a field and bend R, through a series of gates to a fantastic view over the Caldew and the estates of Hawksdale Hall. Through several fields the earth track becomes tarmac. Bear L at the next opportunity down a bridleway signed for Raughtonhead Hill. Follow this track across the road in front of Lime House School to descend over the River Caldew. Climb to take the next R, climbing steeply again to tarmac at Raughtonhead Hill Farm. Emerge at a T-junction and L to rejoin the on-road route.

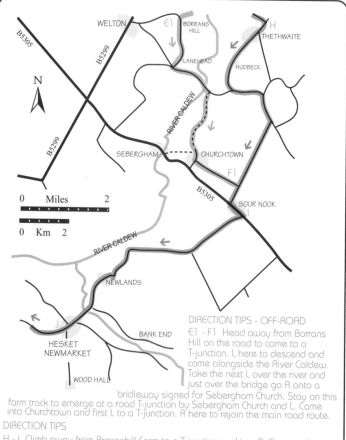

Traditional Eden Valley house in Burgh by Sands (section 6)

7 HESKET NEWMARKET - WHITEHAVEN

Section Distance 36.5 miles / 59km

Off-road About 18 miles using all off-road options.

The Route Once over the corner of the Caldbeck and Uldale Fells the route enters what is generally a long and steady descent towards the finish, although some small, stiff climbs remain, for example out of Workington. If you want to break this long section down into two easier days Cockermouth is an excellent place to do so, with its historic sights and convenient services. The first main off-road option follows what can be a quagmire of a track shortly after passing through Bassenthwaite so is for DRY SUMMER WEATHER ONLY. The second, over Watch Hill, is on a good track but involves a long climb.

HESKET NEWMARKET TO COCKERMOUTH

• The **Caldbeck Fells** are one of the quieter corners of the Lake District National Park. This northern tip, however, houses some superb scenery. Further west the views over the **Uldale Fells** from the upland plateau approaching Longlands are almost unearthly and are followed by glimpses of **Bassenthwaite Lake** as you descend towards Cockermouth.
• The first major off-road option passes through **Bassenthwaite** village. Whitewashed houses cluster idyllically around a beck at the foot of the massive Skiddaw peak. The **Sun** and **Castle Inns** are handy watering holes. Two to three kilometres before the village look out for the spectacular **Dash Beck** waterfall up to the left.

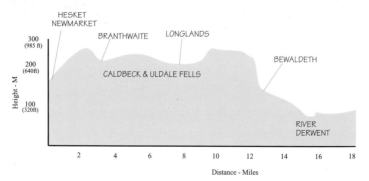

HESKET NEWMARKET TO COCKERMOUTH - ACCOMMODATION

Swaledale Watch, Whelpo nr Caldbeck (016974) 78409
The Snooty Fox, Uldale (016973) 71479. About 2km off the route.
Kiln Hill Farm, nr Bassenthwaite (017687) 76454
Lakeside Guest House, Dubwath nr Bassenthwaite Lake (017687) 76358.
££££(£)-PL-DR-SEC. Self-catering lodge also available.
▲ **Robin Hood Caravan Park**, nr Bassenthwaite (017687) 76334. Open April
-November.

Bassenthwaite village (section 7, off-road option)

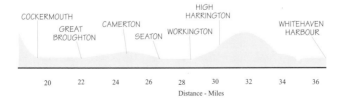

COCKERMOUTH - HISTORY AND ATTRACTIONS

• One of only two listed '**Gem Towns**' in Cumbria (Whitehaven is the other). See map opposite to locate the numbered attractions below:

1 Wordsworth House. Home of William and Dorothy Wordsworth. National Trust owned with cafe. Admission fee to non-members. Seasonal variations in opening. (01900) 824805
2 Printing House Museum. Unusual display of printing technology through the ages. 'Hands on' experience. Admission charge. (01900) 824984
3 Aspects of Motoring Museum. Motoring through the ages. Admission charge. Closed Jan. Restricted opening Feb. (01900) 824448. **Jennings Brewery Tour**. Working brewery. No charge. (01900) 823214.
4 Toy and Model Museum. Admission charge. Open Feb-Nov. (01900) 827606
5 Statue of R.Mayo in main street. Former town MP and only Viceroy of India ever assassinated.
6 Castle (private residence)
7 All Saints Church
8 Mining Museum The Creighton Mineral Collection has stones of beautiful shape and colour. Also old mining artefacts. April - December. Small admission charge.(01900) 828301.

COCKERMOUTH - ACCOMMODATION

Rook Guest House, 9 Castlegate (01900) 828496 £££-PL-DR-LAU-SEC.
Castlegate Guest House 6 Castlegate (01900) 826749 £££-PL-LAU-SEC.
Rose Cottage, Lorton Rd (01900) 822189. £££(£)-ME-PL-DR-LAU-SEC.
Albany House Wordsworth Terrace, Windmill Lane (01900) 825630
££££-PL-DR-LAU-SEC. 0.5km.
Benson Court Cottage, 10 St Helens St. (01900) 822303 ££-DR-LAU nearby-SEC. Very near route.
The Old Vicarage, Lorton Rd (01900) 828505 £££-SEC-WKSH. 3.75 miles.
Croft House, 8 Challoner Street (01900) 822532
Emoh Ruo, 2 Willow Lane (01900) 822951
Globe Hotel, Main Street (01900) 822126
Cockermouth Youth Hostel, Double Mills (01900) 822561. Evening meal, self-catering, cycle shed, all day access. ££.
△ **Wyndham Holiday Park**, Old Keswick Road, Cockermouth (01900) 822571. Open March-November. **Violet Bank Caravan Park**, Simonscales Lane, Cockermouth (01900) 822169. March-November.

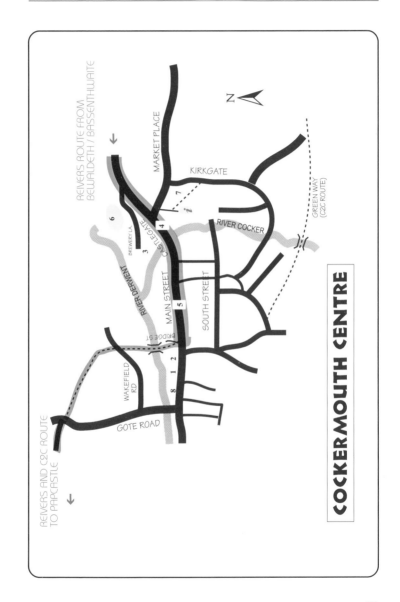

COCKERMOUTH - OTHER INFORMATION

Tourist Information Town Hall, Market St. (01900) 822634
Market Days Monday including livestock auction.
Early Closing Thursday
Hospital Cockermouth Cottage Hospital (01900) 822226. Minor injuries only.
For broken bones or more serious illness contact West Cumberland Hospital
near Whitehaven (see page 80).
Banks Barclays, 30 Main St. Cashpoint. - Midland, 1 Main St. Cashpoint.
℞ **Wordsworth Hotel Bike Hire** (01900) 822757 **Derwent Cycles**, 4 Market
Place (01900) 822113

COCKERMOUTH TO WHITEHAVEN

• **Papcastle** Site of a former Roman Fort, now a pretty village with many of its
houses being one or two hundred years old. **The Bird in Hand** is the village
pub.
• **Great Broughton** Christchurch pretty village church. Several pubs plus village
store and fish and chip shop!
• **Camerton** Main buildings are St Peter's Church and Camerton Hall, which is
about half a kilometre to the west of the centre. **Black Tom Inn** (no meals).
• **Workington** Still retains a working port dominated by industry but the once-
famed coal, steel and shipbuilding has all but gone. The **Helena Thompson
Museum** is based on the bequest of the eponymous local worthy and also
includes displays on Workington's social and industrial history in a fine Georgian
building. Free admission. (01900) 62598. **Workington Hall** Is an imposing ruin
and home of the former Lords of the Manor, the Curwens. Admission charge.
(01900) 604351. ℞ **Traffic Lights Bikes**, 35 Washington St. (01900) 603283.
The Bike Bank, 18-20 Market Place (01900) 603337.

COCKERMOUTH TO WHITEHAVEN - ACCOMMODATION

Osborne House, 31 Brow Top, Workington (01900) 603400. ££-PL-DR-LAU-
SEC
The Boston, 1 St Michaels Rd, Workington (01900) 603435. ££(£)-PL-DR-
SEC.
Morven House Hotel, Siddick Rd. Workington (01900) 602118 £££-PL-DR-
LAU-SEC-WKSH. Meal available.
Sunny House, Asby nr. Workington (01946) 861934 ££-PL-DR-SEC-WKSH.
Appletree Inn, 31 Finkle St. Workington (01900) 871160 ££-ME(Pub attached)-
PL-DR-SEC-WKSH.
Sandmands Guest House, 123 John St. Workington (01900) 605763
Glenlea, Glenlea Hill, Lowca. (01946) 693873. £££-ME-PL-DR-LAU-SEC.

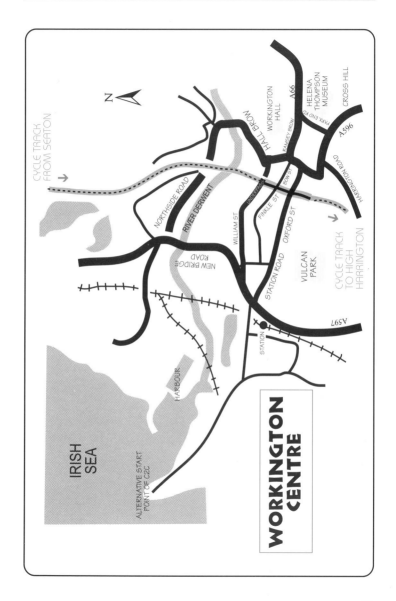

WHITEHAVEN - HISTORY AND ATTRACTIONS

• Listed **Gem Town**, with well-preserved Georgian architecture. Unusual gridiron street pattern made Whitehaven the first planned town since the middle ages. Many fine buildings. See Roper St. and Lowther St. for good examples.
• Interesting **harbour area** with nearby mine remains of Wellington and Duke Pits at South Beach Recreation Area (2). Candlestick Chimney (1) viewpoint part of former Wellington pit (operating 1840-1932). Scene of 1910 mine disaster with 136 lives lost.
• The **Beacon Museum** (3) showing the town's connection with slavery, smuggling, mining, shipbuilding and America. Met. Office weather gallery and views over the Solway Firth. Admission charge. (01946) 592302.
• **Michael Moon's Bookshop**, Roper St. - huge selection of second-hand books.
• **St. Jame's Church** has a fine Georgian interior (5). St. Nicholas Church consists of a fine tower on Lowther St. (4) Drinks and snacks some weekends.

WHITEHAVEN - ACCOMMODATION

Glenard Guest House, Inkerman Terrace (01946) 692249 ££-ME-PL-DR-SEC-WKSH.
Lismore Guest House, Wellington Row (01946) 66028 ££-PL-DR-LAU-SEC.
Tarn Flatt Hall, Sandwith (01946) 692162   B&B-£££ Camping Barn-£3-ME PL(with B&B only)-DR-SEC.
Tivoli Guest House, 156 Queen St (01946) 67400 ££-PL-SEC.
Cross Georgian Guest House, Sneckyeat Rd, Henshingham (01946) 63716 ££(£)-PL-SEC. 1 mile from start. Long stay parking available.
Brunos Hotel, 9-11 Church St. (01946) 65270
Corkickle Guest House, 1 Corkickle (01946) 692073
Waverley Hotel, Tangier St. (01946) 694337

WHITEHAVEN - OTHER FACILITIES

Tourist Information Market Hall, Market Place (01946) 695678
Market Days Thursday and Saturday
Hospital West Cumberland Hospital, Henshingham (01946) 693181
Banks Barclays Bank, Strand St. Cashpoint - Midland Bank, 69 Lowther St. Cashpoint - NatWest, 71 Lowther St. Cashpoint
ۻ Mark Taylor Cycles, 5-6 New St. (01946) 692252 Camskill Cycles, Pottery Rd. , off Coach Rd. (01946) 694794

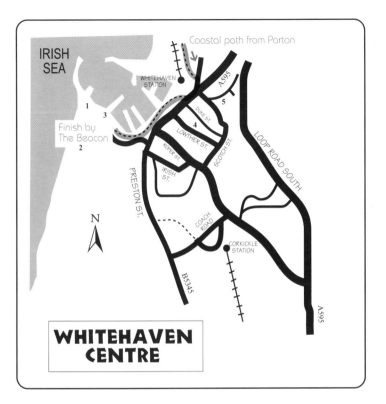

Coastal path from Parton

IRISH SEA

WHITEHAVEN STATION

A595

DUKE ST.

1
3

Finish by The Beacon
2

LOWTHER ST.

ROPER ST.

IRISH ST.

SCOTCH ST.

LOOP ROAD SOUTH

4

5

PRESTON ST.

N

COACH ROAD

CORKICKLE STATION

B5345

A595

WHITEHAVEN CENTRE

BACK UP SERVICES (FROM PAGE 12)

Holiday Lakeland Breakdown support, luggage transfer, cycle hire and complete holiday service. (016973) 71871.

Tyne Valley Holidays Luggage transfer, cycle hire, holiday service. (0191) 2847534.

Kielder Bikes, Kielder Castle (01434) 250392. Rescue service, cycle hire.

Secure Compound Parking, Workington (01900) 604997. Cycle lock up and long-term parking.

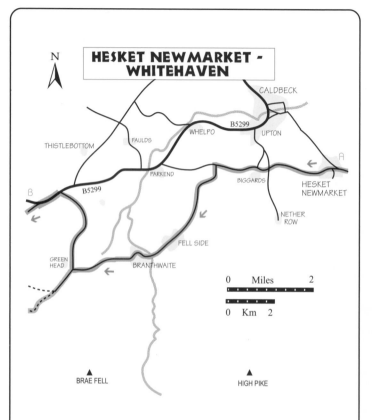

HESKET NEWMARKET - WHITEHAVEN

N

CALDBECK

B5299

WHELPO

UPTON

FAULDS

THISTLEBOTTOM

PARKEND

A

B5299

BIGGARDS

HESKET
NEWMARKET

B

NETHER
ROW

FELL SIDE

GREEN
HEAD

BRANTHWAITE

| 0 | Miles | 2 |
| 0 | Km | 2 |

▲
BRAE FELL

▲
HIGH PIKE

DIRECTION TIPS

A - B Stay on the main road past the green in Hesket Newmarket, then take the first L. 1.5km out of Hesket Newmarket pass the L for Nether Row and the R for Upton and Caldbeck. Take the next L signed for Fell Side and Branthwaite. Pass through both these tiny farming hamlets (just over 1km out of Branthwaite a road marked as a dead end on the L is the off-road link to Longlands). Continue to a T-junction with the B5299 and L for Mealsgate and Aspatria. Stay on this road, ignoring the next R turn, in effect leaving the B5299.

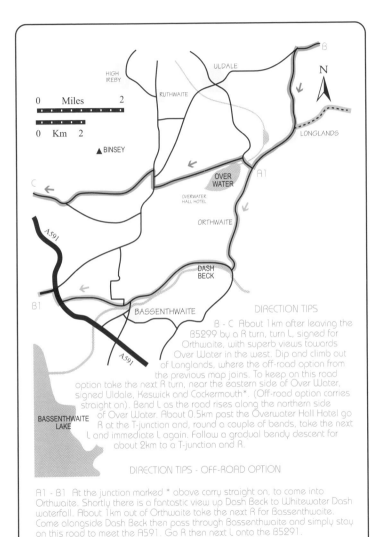

DIRECTION TIPS

B - C About 1km after leaving the B5299 by a R turn, turn L, signed for Orthwaite, with superb views towards Over Water in the west. Dip and climb out of Longlands, where the off-road option from the previous map joins. To keep on this road option take the next R turn, near the eastern side of Over Water, signed Uldale, Keswick and Cockermouth*. (Off-road option carries straight on). Bend L as the road rises along the northern side of Over Water. About 0.5km past the Overwater Hall Hotel go R at the T-junction and, round a couple of bends, take the next L and immediate L again. Follow a gradual bendy descent for about 2km to a T-junction and R.

DIRECTION TIPS - OFF-ROAD OPTION

A1 - B1 At the junction marked * above carry straight on, to come into Orthwaite. Shortly there is a fantastic view up Dash Beck to Whitewater Dash waterfall. About 1km out of Orthwaite take the next R for Bassenthwaite. Come alongside Dash Beck then pass through Bassenthwaite and simply stay on this road to meet the A591. Go R then next L onto the B5291.

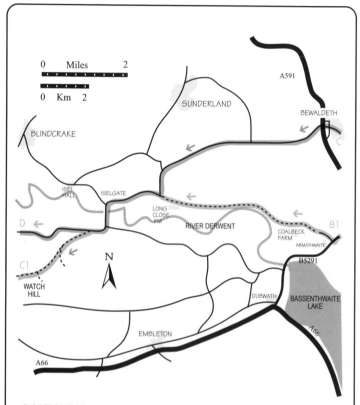

DIRECTION TIPS

C - D Head on the road through Bewaldeth to a junction with the A591.
Go straight over this main road and stay on the long straight sections of the
next road for about 4km to come to a T-junction. Go L marked for Cockermouth
(soon off-road option joins from the track on L for Long Close Farm). At the
next T-junction in the valley bottom go L marked for Keswick and Cockermouth
and immediately cross over the Derwent. Climb to the next T-junction and R
for Cockermouth. The off-road option splits off to the L but the road option
stays on the tarmac here.

DIRECTION TIPS - OFF-ROAD OPTION

B1 - C1 On the B5291 pass the Castle Inn at the junction with the A591 and in front of the Armathwaite Hall Hotel go R, marked as a dead end. Pass Coalbeck Farm and at the R-hand bend ignore the footpath signed to the R and carry straight on, onto the rough bridleway for Isel (3 miles). NOTE - this bridleway can be VERY MUDDY after rain and throughout the winter. The track comes alongside the River Derwent in this beautiful valley bottom. Follow the track through a gate and over a beck, staying alongside the river with conifer forest up to your R. The track climbs to join a tarmac road through Long Close Farm and comes to a T-junction. L here to descend for just over a kilometre to another T-junction and L over the River Derwent. Climb to the next T-junction and go R for Cockermouth. In about 250m go L up a well-surfaced bridleway track that skirts the bottom side of a plantation. Ignore the first split L and after about 2km of ascent, including some steep climbing, the track appears to hairpin back into the woods. Head through the gate on your R and onto the grassy track on the R-hand side of a large field.

Whitehaven harbour slipway, near the end of the route (section 7)

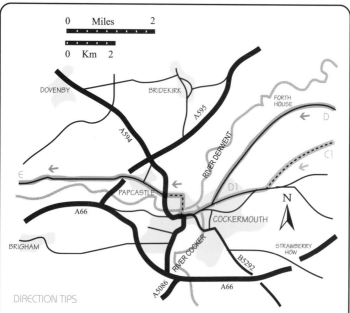

DIRECTION TIPS

D - E After turning R above the Derwent (see previous map) simply follow the road for about 5km to come into Cockermouth. At the T-junction by Links sports centre turn R into the town centre. Head along Main Street.* About 30m past the United Reformed Church go R down Bridge Street (you are now also following C2C signs). Cross the bridge over the Derwent and go R onto the road. In about 15-20m split L onto a path that leads behind a football field to the main A594. Cross this BUSY AND FAST road, and continue into Papcastle. Ignore any turnings heading through Papcastle and exit the village to go over a bridge above the A595.

DIRECTION TIPS - OFF-ROAD OPTION

C1 - D1 On the grassy summit of Watch Hill continue on the grass track down the R-hand side of the field. There are superb views over Lorton Vale and the massed peaks surrounding it, over to your L. Keep on the line of this track as it descends through several fields for about 1.5km to finally bend L and join the road. Go R and follow the road into Cockermouth, avoiding any turnings until you descend onto Main Street. From here pick up the directions at the point marked * above.

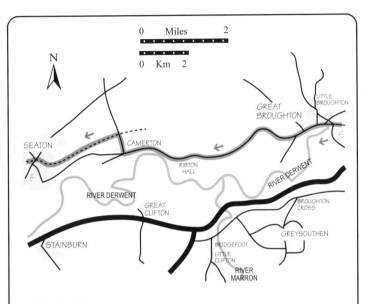

DIRECTION TIPS

E - F Head away from Papcastle, with the River Derwent down to your L. At the edge of Great Broughton hit a junction and go R up Harris Brow (not the most immediate R). Head through Great Broughton centre past the Punch Bowl Inn. Before the R bend onto Moor Road go L onto West End. Stay on this road out of Great Broughton and in about 4km enter Camerton. At the T-junction by the Black Tom Inn go R and climb steeply. At the old stone bridge at the top of this climb go L onto the well-surfaced cycle track. Follow the track through countryside then through Seaton.

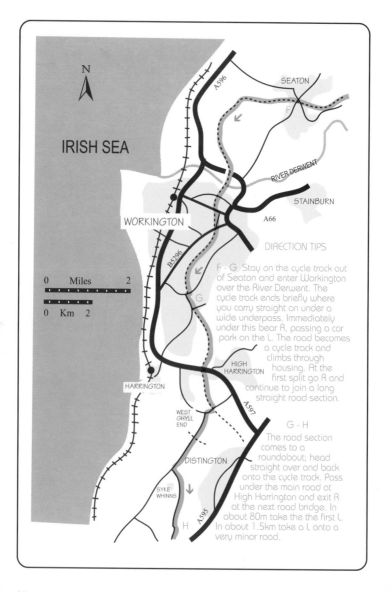

IRISH SEA

WORKINGTON

0 Miles 2

0 Km 2

HARRINGTON

WEST
GHYLL
END

SYKE
WHINNS

A596

SEATON

RIVER DERWENT

STAINBURN

A66

DISTINGTON

A595

A597

HIGH
HARRINGTON

B5296

DIRECTION TIPS

F - G Stay on the cycle track out of Seaton and enter Workington over the River Derwent. The cycle track ends briefly where you carry straight on under a wide underpass. Immediately under this bear R, passing a car park on the L. The road becomes a cycle track and climbs through housing. At the first split go R and continue to join a long straight road section.

G - H The road section comes to a roundabout; head straight over and back onto the cycle track. Pass under the main road at High Harrington and exit R at the next road bridge. In about 80m take the the first L. In about 1.5km take a L onto a very minor road.

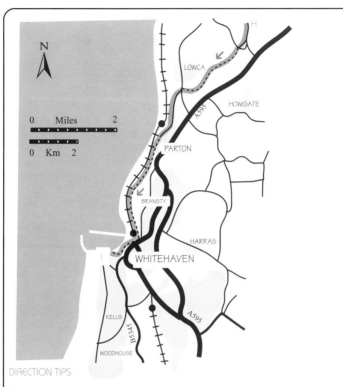

DIRECTION TIPS

H - I Shortly after passing Blackett Holme farm buildings on the L pass by the remains of an old railway bridge. Immediately past these turn R onto an excellent cycle track. Cross over a minor road and continue into Lowca. Join a rougher track by nurseries, down to the L. Very shortly cut L onto the cycle track and to a T-junction with West Croft Terrace. Descend on this fast road and in about 300m take the next R signed for Parton. Pass the PO and village hall and before the steep climb go R down Bank Yard Road. This road turns into a beautiful coastal track with only the railway separating you from the sea. Follow the track to a T-junction with Bransty Road in Whitehaven. Go R to come immediately to another T-junction and R again. At the start of Tangier Street jink R then L to follow the path in front of the harbour and round to The Beacon (see centre map for more detail).

INDEX
CITIES, TOWNS, VILLAGES & PLACES IN MAIN TEXT

Entries in red type indicate town maps

ACCOMMODATION / CAMPING INDEX

Δ   at the end of an accommodation section indicates camping facilities

ABOUT THE AUTHOR

Richard Peace is a freelance author and photographer. He was educated at Queen Elizabeth Grammar School, Wakefield and Magdalen College, Oxford. After several periods of foreign travel he qualified as a solicitor and began outdoor writing as a hobby during his time in a solicitor's office. He has eleven titles to his name. He has also written for several national outdoor magazines.

OTHER BOOKS BY RICHARD PEACE

All guides are illustrated with either drawings or photos and come complete with sketch maps and lots of other practical information.

CYCLING GUIDES

THE ULTIMATE C2C GUIDE £6.95 ISBN 1-901464-02-4
Excellent Books
Simply the most popular long distance cycling route in the UK, completed by thousands each year. From the Cumbrian coast to Newcastle or Sunderland.

YORKSHIRE DALES CYCLE WAY £5.50 ISBN 1-870141-28-8
Hillside Publications
An outstanding 130 mile route circling the entire national park. Beginning in the market town of Skipton. Malham, Settle, Dent, and Swaledale precede a superb return to Grassington. Minor roads follow leafy dales and cross open moorland.

WEST YORKSHIRE CYCLE WAY £4.99 ISBN 1-870141-38-5
Hillside Publications
This 152 mile route starts in Haworth and takes in many of the contrasts of West Yorkshire, from pastoral plains to rolling Pennine scenery. Visit Otley Chevin, Pontefract Castle, Aberford and the Worth and Holme Valleys.

MOUNTAIN BIKING WEST AND SOUTH YORKSHIRE £5.99
ISBN 1-870141-40-7 Hillside Publications
20 rides, 8.5 to 16.5 miles, from the high Pennines to the rolling eastern plains. Includes Ilkley Moor, Calderdale, Holme Valley and Barnsley Canal.

THE ULTIMATE WEST COUNTRY WAY GUIDE £8.95
ISBN 1-901464-03-2 Excellent Books
152 pages packed with information and pictures on this 250 mile Sustrans route through the best of the south-west.

BIKING COUNTRY GLASGOW, CLYDE VALLEY AND LOCH LOMOND £5.99
ISBN 1-870141-45-8 Hillside Publications
18 well-researched and attractive routes exploring the hidden corners around Glasgow. Using canal towpaths, special cycle tracks, farm tracks and minor roads, the routes range from 6 to 18 miles.

MOUNTAIN BIKE LANCASHIRE AND SOUTH PENNINES £5.99
ISBN 1-901464-00-8 Excellent Books
20 off-road routes, visiting numerous scenic highlights in the Red Rose County and South Pennines. 6.5 to 20 miles to suit all levels of mountain biker. Includes famed scenery such as the Bowland Fells and Pendle Witch Country.

LEISURE RIDES IN THE PEAK DISTRICT AND DERBYSHIRE £5.95
ISBN 1-901464-01-6 Excellent Books
25 trails and circular routes in the Peak District and Derbyshire. Ideal for families and occasional / leisure riders. Many moderate length outings with longer linear outings allowing you to do as much or as little as you like. Practical advice on cycling with children plus cycle hire and eating details. Routes cover the Dark and the White Peak areas and visitor attractions such as Chatsworth.

WALKING AND GENERAL GUIDES

YORK WALKS £2.50 ISBN 1-870141-47-4 Hillside Publications
5 classic walks around the city of York exploring the major tourist sites and many lesser known features. Each theme walk traces an aspect of the York story over the centuries. Includes children's attractions and historic inns.

THE MACLEHOSE TRAIL AND ITS SURROUNDINGS £7.99
ISBN 962-7335-14-2 The Alternative Press, Hong Kong
Written during the author's period in Hong Kong teaching English, this is a complete practical guide to the superb 100 kilometre walking trail that crosses the mountainous New Territories of Hong Kong. A superb blend of cityscape and wild countryside add up to a once in-a-lifetime experience.

LANCASHIRE CURIOSITIES £6.95
ISBN 1-874336-42-3 The Dovecote Press
This popular series from the Dovecote Press looks at follies, buildings and all things curious on a county by county basis. 80 interesting sites county-wide, profusely illustrated with quality black and white photographs.

THE ABOVE BOOKS MAY BE OBTAINED AT ALL GOOD BOOK SHOPS OR DIRECT FROM EXCELLENT BOOKS (DETAILS AT FRONT OF BOOK).

OTHER NEW TITLES FOR 1999

THE LONDON TO OXFORD CLASSIC (Includes an interim version of Sustrans' Thames Valley Cycle Route) OUT NOW PRICE £7.95   *ISBN 1-901464-04-0*

An entirely new route for 1999 linking arguably the two finest cities in the country via 200 miles of glorious cycling. The Thames Valley Cycle Route combines the quiet grandeur of the Thames with the rural charm of South-East Oxfordshire before your arrival in the incomparable city of Oxford. The return leg visits many beauty spots in the northern Chilterns before joining the Grand Union Canal and a number of other off-road cycle trails, taking you back to the Thames in central London. Lots of good quality off-road riding and quiet minor roads escape the traffic to make this an ideal family challenge as well as an exciting ride for two-wheeled tourists from near and far.

PRICE £7.95   ISBN 1-901464-04-0

THE ULTIMATE DEVON COAST TO COAST GUIDE
£5.95 (ESTIMATED)   ISBN 1-901464-06-7
ESTIMATED RELEASE JUNE 99

A southern coast to coast ride from Ilfracombe to Plymouth linking the Plym Valley and Tarka trails and visiting Dartmoor and the rolling green hills of north Devon on the way. 90 miles.

WANT TO KNOW MORE ABOUT SUSTRANS!

Full details of other Sustrans routes and a catalogue of their route maps, other products and subscription details are available by dialling their public information line on (0117) 9290888.